Voodoo Science Park convincingly demonstrates that history is only ever rewritten and that there can consequently be little room for 'accidents' in any of our accepted historical accounts. If this text overturns all orthodox readings of the documented past, it does so simply in the name of prophecy, the authors being bold enough to let the existing state of affairs speak for itself. Such eloquent restraint is extremely rare, extracting a simple yet undeniable poetry from the unearthing of connections between events. Through this gently persistent accumulation of facts, an enigmatic half-hidden landscape is gradually transformed into the starkest of mythologies.
Ken Hollings, Author of *Welcome to Mars*

Combining compelling archive with contemporary footage of the Health and Safety Laboratory in the Peak District, Derbyshire, Voodoo Science Park *summons the poetic and political archetypes of Leviathan, Albion and Gogmagog in order to anatomise the powers of accident, reenactment, sacrifice, punishment, artificial life, magic, sleep and civil war in the state of Britain. Part video-essay, video-poem and video-guide,* Voodoo Science Park *is a vivid and erudite conjuration that redreams the history of our present with a passion and a purpose that is entirely visionary.*
Kodwo Eshun, The Otolith Group
on the film-of-the-book

Here maverick theorist Steve Beard, working with Victoria Halford, fashions a fascinating, Keiller-esque meditation on Hobbes's Leviathan, *the covert geographies of Albion and post-Ballardian crash theory.*
Sukhdev Sandhu, Author of *London Calling: How Black and Asian Writers Imagined A City*
on the film-of-the-book

T0066500

Voodoo Science Park

Voodoo
Science Park

Victoria Halford

and

Steve Beard

Winchester, UK
Washington, USA

First published by Zero Books, 2011
Zero Books is an imprint of John Hunt Publishing Ltd., Laurel House, Station Approach,
Alresford, Hants, SO24 9JH, UK
office1@o-books.net
www.o-books.com

For distributor details and how to order please visit the 'Ordering' section on our website.

Text copyright: Victoria Halford and Steve Beard 2010

ISBN: 978 1 84694 527 4

A CIP catalogue record for this book is available from the British Library.

Design: Stuart Davies

Printed in the UK by CPI Antony Rowe
Printed in the USA by Offset Paperback Mfrs, Inc

We operate a distinctive and ethical publishing philosophy in all
areas of our business, from our global network of authors to
production and worldwide distribution.

CONTENTS

for
Ken & Dawn
and
Sarah

"The chronicle is the expression of the irreversible time of power and also the instrument that preserves the voluntaristic progression of this time from its predecessor, since this orientation of time collapses with the fall of every specific power and returns to the indifferent oblivion of cyclical time, the only time known to peasant masses who, during the collapse of empires and their chronologies, never change."

Guy Debord, *Society of the Spectacle*

Preface

Voodoo Science Park started life as a film about the science of accident investigation as it is conducted at the Health and Safety Laboratory in Buxton, Derbyshire. This is the place where large-scale accidents – such as fires, explosions, tunnel collapses, bridge failures and rail crashes – are recreated to examine their destructive pathways.

The scenario for our film is simple. It is that accident investigation, with its practices of reconstruction and imitation, shares an affinity with the rituals of sympathetic magic or voodoo. According to this idea, the accident victim becomes a designated social sacrifice.

We wrote a script for the film which imagined an atemporal encounter in the Peak District of Derbyshire between the political philosopher and proto-scientist Thomas Hobbes and the poet and prophet William Blake. Hobbes lived in the Peak District for most of his life as a kind of hanger-on at one of the great feudal households. In 1626, he wrote an estate poem for his lord called *The Wonders of the Peak*, which we used as a jumping-off point for structuring our film's narrative. The narrator of the film is "Blakey", an outsider who carries memories of William Blake's own dissident views. Our voicescript is included in the "Film Documents" section at the back of this book.

"Notes on a Film Scenario" present the research findings which went into the making of our film. These notes are attached to trigger phrases grabbed from the film's voicescript, which now behave almost as if they were chapter titles. The notes are sequenced to deliver the shape of a narrative and perhaps, even, an argument. They include ruminations on Hobbes and his theory of the state, Blake's shamanistic visions, the industrial safety rigs in the grounds of the Health and Safety

Laboratory and the psychogeography of the Peak District landscape, considered as a kind of "accident blackspot" modelling forms of social persecution. These notes can be read in any order, but they benefit from being read from beginning to end. They were written by Steve Beard, who bears sole responsibility for any errors.

Victoria Halford and Steve Beard
Hove, March 2010

Foreword

by Stewart Home

Voodoo Science Park (VSP)'s synthesis of fiction and non-fiction is so subtle that it is perhaps the best example yet of what the Italian fiction collective Wu Ming call an "unidentified narrative object" (UNO); something that might be crudely understood as docu-fiction. Both the film and text accompanying *VSP* extend the range and depth of a specifically English psychogeography developed in the 1990s by individuals such as Richard Essex and Andy Jordan, who used occult theories about ley-lines to map out their own subjective relationships to urban and non-urban space. *VSP* is set in the Peak District, a National Park that acts as a simulacrum of the countryside in a globalised capitalist world. It should go without saying that there is no longer any real distinction between the country and the city, if there ever was. As the makers of *VSP* note, the Peak District was one of the first places to suffer the enclosure of common lands, and it was the concomitant industrialisation of agriculture that immediately preceded and made possible the expansion of the cities, by freeing up the labour force that became the nascent "urban" proletariat.

The film and accompanying text root the seventeenth-century materialist philosopher Thomas Hobbes in the false landscape of the Peak District. As the *VSP* materials explain at length, Hobbes lived in this geographical location for much of his adult life. Logically then, the *VSP* narrative is spun around Hobbes' poem *De Mirabilibus Pecci* AKA *The Wonders of The Peak,* with his more famous materialist and political works playing a relatively peripheral role. If we are to understand Hobbes as a materialist philosopher, then surely we need to understand how and where he lived. Hobbes' world view finds its contemporary

3

manifestation in the Harpur Hill Health and Safety Laboratory (HSL), which is the central geographical location of *VSP*. The Health and Safety Lab attempts to recreate industrial accidents as a kind of reverse voodoo, in a manner analogous to the way Halford and Beard's film - and in particular the accompanying text - act as a self-consciously post-modern simulacrum and updating of Hobbes' seventeenth-century narrative poem.

Like the verse it corrects and reworks, *VSP* is a self-reflectively subjective map of the Peak District and its history. Working from the assumption that the various stone circles located in this geographical area had an occult function, *VSP* substitutes the Health and Safety Lab for these Neolithic features (which it largely ignores). Science and its occult double are merged in both this government installation and the historical figures of Hobbes and his romantic antithesis William Blake. When the two are brought together we get a glimpse of what it should be like to be truly human. Plainly, full blown and outright romantic rejections of reason are every bit as silly as deifying the rational. What's actually required is the selective employment of analytical and/or correlative thinking as is appropriate to a specific situation, but in capitalist societies the alienated are invited to opt for one or the other. This is a deformation *VSP* rejects.

VSP provides both a historical and a mythological account of the Peak District, but this is not an exhaustive indexing. There are no explicit references to the Phantom Helicopters that some commentators claim plagued Harpur Hill for two years in the mid-1970s[1]. For believers, Phantom Helicopters are connected to Unidentified Flying Objects (UFOs) and alien invasions. If *VSP* were an attempt to fabricate a populist sensation then it would transform HSL and Harpur Hill into the English equivalent of Roswell and Area 51 in the United States, with "military" technicians back-engineering advanced alien spacecraft in secret hangars and performing autopsies on dead extraterrestrials.

Hobbes has far less of a hold on the mass imagination of today than flying saucers, but if we're to understand our alienated society then he's a figure to whom it is useful to return.

Likewise, among the more infamous aspects of relatively recent Peak District history studiously ignored by *VSP* is the use of Saddleworth Moor by the sex killers Ian Brady and Myra Hindley as a burial site for several of the children they murdered in the 1960s. *VSP* understands that all histories and psychogeographies are necessarily subjective, and that by ignoring the more spectacular and obvious imagery associated with the Peak District in general - and Harpur Hill in particular - this emerges all the more effectively in the telling of a tale that appears genuinely unfamiliar and strange, but is nonetheless rooted in historical materialism. This is a counter-mythology to X-Files style "history". The "truth" ain't out there, it is socially constructed and we all play a role in this. What *VSP* tells us is that instead of watching the skies we need to return our gaze to the earth. Our broken capitalist society is not going to be fixed by an advanced extraterrestrial civilisation; instead we need to set about transforming it ourselves!

1. For example, see: Clarke, David and Roberts, Andy, *Phantoms of the Sky: UFOs – A Modern Myth?* Robert Hale, London, 1990 pages 55-64.

NOTES ON A FILM SCENARIO

state of emergency – sovereignty as a demonic pact – the scape-goating of Cromwell.

PEAKLAND

The Peak District is an area of high ground in the East Midlands of England. People used to think of its hills as mountains, many years ago. The landscape is extremely varied. In the north, rises the gritstone and moorland, largely cleared of habitation. In the south, are deposited the limestone crags, the wooded valleys and rivers, the tidy little settlements such as Buxton, where most of the human population lives.

The Peak District was declared a National Park by Act of Parliament in 1951. It is England's first National Park. This means that it is an area whose use is highly controlled. It does not mean it is owned by the state. There are areas of the Peak which are owned by national charities but for the most part, the land is privately held, as it has been for centuries.

The signs of possession mark the land in the shape of so many hundreds of drystone walls. They run along the sides of roads, they march across the thin grasslands in columns, they stand against each other and enclose the fields. The walls are stacked about five feet high, the hard grey stones locked into place through a combination of weight, shape and position, with a nine-inch layer of ridged stones sticking out on top. They rise from the land like the spines of half-buried serpents.

Many of these walls were built during the late eighteenth and early nineteenth centuries, with stones partly quarried from the hundreds of Neolithic tombs which litter the Peak. Successive Parliamentary Acts of Enclosure seized control of common lands, judged to be waste, and granted them to the big existing capitalist landowners. These landowners cultivated heather moorlands to act as game reserves, with populations of grouse bred for shooting. They also leased the land to individual tenants, often farmers, who either planted the fields with corn or made them into pasture for sheep. The new tenants built the drystone walls to mark the boundaries of their property, to

protect their assets in the fields, and to keep common people out.

The losers in this new settlement were the old feudal peasants who could not afford the market rents and the cottagers who had earned a subsistence living from the common lands of the Peak. These

01

lands were not waste to them but a native habitat, places where they could cut turf and quarry stones for shelter, grow vegetables and tend cattle, prospect for minerals and go out hunting for rabbits. Evicted from their homes, they often had no choice but to join the sweeping caravans of wandering poor on the roads, where they would have been subject to arbitrary stop and search procedures and other harsh penalties of the criminal code.

Nowadays, people come to the Peak District to admire the scenery. It has a gothic aspect, with its craggy silhouettes and

ridged stonescapes, its antique fortresses and historic ruins. It was artists who showed the way. They were hired by the landowners to document their new properties and they developed conventional ways of seeing the new aesthetic domain of landscape. There was Thomas Smith of Derby, with his "natural prospects", there was the topographical painter Henry Moore, with his map-like

02

views. John Constable briefly stumbled into the Peak to sketch a few scenes and it was a stopping point on J. M. W. Turner's painting tours.

John Ruskin, the art critic and social reformer, came to

Matlock Bath in the 1820s and 1830s and popularised the idea that the landscape aesthetic could tame and improve the mind of the observer. The development of the railways from the 1840s to the 1860s made the Peak District newly accessible and towards the end of the nineteenth century, factory workers downed tools at the weekend and poured into the area from the surrounding towns of Manchester, Derby, Birmingham and Sheffield. They formed walking guilds and cycling groups, they chalked details of popular tours on factory gates. They called themselves "ramblers".

It's tempting to think of the rambler in the English countryside as the less celebrated cousin of that heroic modernist figure – the dandy in Paris. The French sociologist Michel de Certeau praises the dandy for his virtuosity in wandering through the city in ways which subvert the fixed views of the urban planners, opening up new ways of moving and thinking, of dressing and connecting. This is something launched by the gutter odysseys of Charles Baudelaire, adopted by the flea-market hauntings of the surrealists and finally abandoned to the public through the street sloganeering of the situationists.

The English ramblers had a different experience as they wandered through the Peak District. These wayward factory workers soon discovered that there were no pioneering acts of mobility expected of them. If they strayed off the public footpaths, then the gamekeepers of the big estates would descend the hills and harass them with their dogs. Jumping over a drystone wall into a private field was not just a poetic act of subversion. It also revived memories of older acts of transgression, when poachers would be hanged for stealing a sheep.

In April 1932, a group of ramblers walked on to the mossy plateau of Kinder Scout, high in the north of the Peak District, in a deliberate act of mass trespass. They were arrested by the police and six were imprisoned for "riotous assembly". In

September 1932, a similar act of trespass occurred at Abbey Brook in a show of solidarity with the imprisoned ramblers. In most cases, the tactical objectives of the ramblers were limited to reclaiming access rights to ancient footpaths. They had no counter-strategy to oppose to the strategy of land enclosures which had already been in place for 150 years and more.

These encounters with the landscape were politically transformative for the ramblers. They escaped the aesthetic of the sublime encounter handed down by romantics such as Ruskin. Instead, they were direct encounters with the repressive power of the state. At such shocking moments, as the surrealist mystic Walter Benjamin affirms, a hidden view of the past can rise up in the minds of those affected in a sudden flash of illumination.

03

In this instance, there would have been a connection with a secret history of popular sedition, buried in the folklore of Dick Turpin and Robin Hood, Queen Mab and the Green Man. There would have been a vision of men and women in masks of green leaves, travelling in packs on the roads at night, holding burning torches and improvised weapons. They demolished the drystone walls, pulled up the corn in the fields, laid open the bellies of sheep and placed hexes on the gates of the landowners.

Benjamin's idea of the secular illumination draws on theories of ancestral memory. It is indeed the case that many of the ramblers in the Peak were descended from those evicted from common land, travellers on the highways, families whose children eventually found new lives as wage labourers in the industrial cities. The holiday jaunts of the ramblers were in that sense scattered raids conducted on territory which had once belonged to their own people.

Perhaps it's not fanciful to open up Benjamin's idea and think more widely about landscape imprinted by the psychic traces of strongly felt collective events, ranging from the trauma of exile to the ecstasy of communion. Under such circumstances it might be possible for anyone to pick up these traces again, long after the events have lapsed into oblivion, when they have slipped from the official archives, and become no more than stories told by children, or voices echoing from the rocks.

It is simply a matter of finding the right technique.

CHURCH OF ALBION

The history of modernity in the Peak District is also the history of the growth in state power and the decline in religious dissent. The Peak was once famous for its radical sects, from the Methodists of the eighteenth century back to the Quakers and Baptists of the seventeenth century. The crucible for the accelerated development of the dissident religious mindset was the English Civil War.

The Quakers and Baptists belonged to a stratum of popular consciousness which raised God's law over the law of the state and followed promptings which it's claimed were divinely guided. There were the Adamites and the Muggletonians, the Seekers and the Ranters. There were the Diggers and the Fifth Monarchists. There were also rumours of a Church of Albion. Its cunning men preached at Baslow, Wirksworth, Bakewell, Monyash, Bradwell, Eyam and Aldsworth. They brought the rain with them. People broke down and wept at their words, gave away their worldly goods and ran naked through the streets.

During the reign of the absolute monarch King Charles I, religious sects were persecuted because they broke the state monopoly on divine access enjoyed by the Church of England. According to a version of the political theology of Jean Bodin, the absolute monarch was granted a divine right to rule by God and this right was devolved to the bishops of the state church. Religious sects, with their talk of a New Jerusalem, a heaven on earth, offered an alternative model of sacred society to that of the absolutist state and their prophets and charismatic leaders obscurely challenged the divine right of the king to rule.

The Peak was a remote place difficult for officers of the state to penetrate. Preachers and religious sects fled to the district. They marshalled enormous popular energies, perhaps drawing on the psychic traces of history embedded in the landscape. Here was a reservoir of troubled feelings for capitalists and Puritan revolutionaries to draw on in their struggle against the king and his reactionary Catholic cronies and feudal landowners. These sectarians were the third force in the Civil War, conjuring prophetic visions from the pages of the Bible and strange ideas from recently translated bodies of alchemical lore.

The religious dissidents were Gnostic Christians who believed that Jesus and the Devil were primarily states of mind and that imagination was the human existence itself. Their most radical proposition was that all private property should be abolished, with people sharing all goods in common. If enacted, it would have meant the tearing down of the drystone walls of the Peak District and the seizure of the governing apparatus of the state. Was this communism or anarchy? Oliver Cromwell and the leaders of the revolutionary party in the Civil War were in no mood to find out.

Once the Civil War was over, monarchist estates had been sequestered by capitalists and the enclosure of common lands was firmly back on the political agenda. The head of King Charles I had been cut off and with this act the whole idea of the divine right of kings had died for good. The troublesome radical sects were now expendable and their leaders could be safely put down. George Fox of the Quakers, for example, was charged with blasphemy and jailed at Derby in 1650 without ever being brought to trial.

By the time Charles's son was installed as a figurehead monarch in the so-called "Restoration" of 1660, the state was firmly atheistic and the Church of England had become a property firm with a nice side-line in religious ceremonies.

The religious sects were persecuted even more severely by the state during the reign of King Charles II. Their divinely inspired enthusiasms were now judged breaches of the civil peace, disturbances, coded acts of war. Acts of Parliament were passed to compel sectarians to renounce their faith and join the

Church of England, or face exile from the offices of public life. Police officers entered the Peak District with crews of soldiers. They broke up congregations and dragged their members to jail. Chapels were destroyed and preachers arrested and fined. Worshippers were forced to meet secretly in pubs, cottages and barns. They massed in the open fields.

The Church of Albion retreated for their religious observances to the isolated Neolithic tombs of the Peak. These spaces had been created between huge limestone slabs, the earth scraped up and the turf moulded to create long, steep barrows. The Church of England had once declared these places taboo, haunts of the Devil. The members of the Church of Albion gathered here to sing Psalms, smoke tobacco and dance around a Maypole covered in green leaves and wild flowers.

04

This religion was stamped out by the state, repressed by its individual members, and retained as a memory perhaps only in the landscape where it occurred.

INTO THE CAVES

The Peak District is a hollow land. Property owners, surveyors and artists have mapped its surface. There lies an undiscovered country beneath. Here is the starting-point for the development of any counter-strategy to the state-backed enclosure of common lands.

The landscape of the Peak is riddled with sink-holes. There are deep cracks running through its limestone strata, like the tunnels of an underground railway system. The fissures intersect to form vast caverns supported by the strong rock. Unseen rivers run through dark passageways. The many caves which score the Peak are the openings into this subterranean network, portals into another dimension.

The shamans of the Upper Paleolithic era understood this other aspect of the Peak. The caves were sacred places for them, gateways to the dead, haunting grounds populated by the totem spirits of the tribe. This is where the shamans came to conduct their ceremonies.

The best preserved of these caves lie north of Ault Hucknall, near Cresswell

05

Crags. Here, there is a limestone ravine whose snaking fissures contain the only prehistoric cave art ever recorded in Britain. Over 80 images have been painted on the walls of Church Hole alone. Other images are found inside the Pin Hole, Robin Hood's Cave and Mother Grundy's Parlour. There are studies of bison and woolly rhinoceroses, their flanks pierced with spears. There are pictures of arctic hares. They were all made by shamans over 10,000 years ago.

06

Imagine the scene. Deep inside the limestone bellies of the caves, separated for a ritual period from their fellows, the shamans took up the red ochre and daubed the walls. They made use of the natural features of the rock walls, the uneven surfaces, to engrave their visions of animal spirits. They were hunting their prey in trance, conjuring the spirits and binding them to the walls, prophesying the good hunting that would follow these rituals.

The painted walls of Church Hole and Mother Grundy's Parlour reveal the elementary principles of sympathetic magic or voodoo. Create an imitation of a desired event, making it so vital that a connection is forged at the elementary level, like calling to like, matter drawing down spirit, copy preceding original. Isolate or bury the effigy so that its magical power is concentrated. Wait at the right place for the anticipated event to occur.

Today it is different. The smaller caves are hidden by foliage and the low-hanging branches of trees, they are padlocked by the local authority, or filled with newspapers and empty soft drink cans. The larger caves around Buxton and Castleton have become tourist attractions, showpiece exhibits, where people go to gaze at the stalagmites dripping from the ceiling and choose from the postcards, while the more adventurous pick their way to the safety barriers at the back and peer into the void.

SINGLE BASTARD FAMILY

Most of the land in the Peak District has for many centuries been owned by a few powerful families. The Duke of Rutland has possessed vast tracts of land. The Duke of Devonshire has also amassed a great territory, encompassing entire villages. The Devonshire title has been passed down the line by generations of the same clan, the Cavendish family, whose power base was consolidated in the Peak District during Elizabethan times by the matriarch, Bess of Hardwick. The influence of the Cavendish family extended throughout the United Kingdom and by the nineteenth century they owned land in eight English counties as well as in Ireland.

The Cavendish clan governed the Peak District on behalf of the British state right up until the enfranchisement of the mass of people in 1832. Even after this, they continued to make their presence felt, by securing through the Church of England's offices the appointment of the local priest, who would also act as the election agent responsible for delivering the local member to Parliament.

07

THOMAS HOBBES

Thomas Hobbes was a scholar fresh out of Oxford University when in 1608 he was employed by the Cavendish family, upon a recommendation from the master of his college, as a tutor and a companion to the 18 year old grandson of Bess of Hardwick. He was 20 years old when he took up this position in the Peak District. He did it for two decades. He left when his master died. Three years later, he was back to teach the elder son of his former pupil, which he did for another seven years. By that time it was 1638. Hobbes was 50 years old.

The late sixteenth and early seventeenth century was an era when old certainties were dying out but new convictions had yet to take their place. This was the interval between feudalism and capitalism, between the universal Christian church of Rome and a national quasi-secular Church of England, between the scholastic philosophy of Oxford and Cambridge universities and the empirical sciences of the Royal Society. It was a gap in history.

The void was filled with various fantastic creations. There was the baroque politics of absolutism, in which a sovereign like King Charles I was thought to be a god. There was the Gnostic religion of the radical sects, some of which, like the Church of Albion, reckoned that the world was created by Satan. And then there was the weird science of alchemy, where adepts such as John Dee sought to transform lead into gold. These manifestations each reached their highest moment of brilliance in the English Civil War, like fireworks, before falling and disappearing into an emptiness.

Hobbes was a creature of this suspended passage through history. He started out at Oxford University when its curriculum was still medieval yet nonetheless managed to end up, a rather cantankerous figure, among the modern scientists of the Royal

Society. In the interval, he was a practitioner of independent thought. This freedom by association was the benefit of getting a job as a hanger-on at one of the great aristocratic families. Hobbes had a room of his own, a library of books, a laboratory of instruments, as well as the opportunity to travel and meet like-minded thinkers.

In 1610, he did the European tour with his young aristocratic companion, having charge of his purse. While the Cavendish heir behaved like a delinquent, Hobbes took the opportunity to meet Galileo Galilei, Johannes

08

Kepler and Pierre Gassendi. Galileo had performed experiments to show that the speed of a falling body is proportional to its density, not its weight. Kepler calculated the motion of planets around the sun. Gassendi was obsessed with the orbit of Mercury and attempted to reconcile the ancient Greek philosophy of atomism with Christianity. Hobbes soaked up the new scientific thinking.

The opportunity afforded by patronage was something perfectly well understood by an earlier generation of Elizabethan scholars. Thomas Hariot stayed first at Durham House in London as part of Sir Walter Raleigh's entourage and then moved to the Petworth estate of the Earl of Northumberland in Sussex. Edward Kelley attached himself to John Dee's Mortlake household in the hope of preferment at court. These men were sometimes called alchemists and magicians. Perhaps it is better to think of them as fabulists on the plane of ideas.

When the English Civil War came in 1642, the Cavendish family naturally sided with King Charles I, as did most of the great aristocratic landowners with any sense of responsibility towards their feudal tenants. The brother of the young man Hobbes had been teaching took up the royal standard and was killed in battle near Newark by Oliver Cromwell's cavalry troop in 1643.

Hobbes had already moved to Paris in 1640. He eventually got another job as a tutor, this time in the exiled royal household of Charles I, where he instructed the king's young son.

Everything changed in 1651, with the publication of Hobbes's great work, *Leviathan*. By this time, Charles I had been decapitated, the Church of England's monopoly on access to divine guidance terminated and Oliver Cromwell was running the country. Hobbes's book argued that the sovereign had no divine right to rule but gained his title from a contract with the people. This would prove an effective rationale for Cromwell's military dictatorship. It permitted the radical religious sects to flourish. But it insulted the memory of Charles I, to the dismay of lingering monarchists (who were busy creating a martyr cult out of the supposedly divine remnants of their dead king).

Hobbes quit Paris in secret and made a dash for London. He was permitted to sink into obscurity by Cromwell's advisors.

Cromwell was busy capitalizing hundreds of thousands of acres of territory. His state had abolished the monarchy and seized control of its land. Much of it was sold off to pay the outstanding wages of the New Model Army and buy their political cooperation. Promises to pay were issued and circulated among the troops. They were bought up by officers at a discount (often of ten percent). When the bills came due, these officers were suddenly landowners and much less inclined to insurrection.

There was an oligarchy of capitalist landowners and big traders ready to take Cromwell's place once he died. What was needed for the sake of appearances was a public figurehead. The son of Charles I, so ably tutored by the atheist Hobbes, was a perfect candidate. He was duly crowned in 1660 amidst the meaningless pageantry of the Restoration, which may well be judged the beginning of the society of the spectacle so despised by situationists. It's no wonder that Charles II, lacking the religious belief of his father, or even the deranged self-belief of Cromwell, should succumb to nihilism and perversity.

One of the things the new king did was to recall Hobbes to court, after spotting his old tutor in the street, and offer him an annual pension of £100, on condition there were no more scandalous books.

In 1675, Hobbes returned to the employ of the Cavendish family in the Peak

09

District. He died from a stroke four years later and his body was carried to the neighbouring church of Ault Hucknall, where he was laid to rest.

SOCIAL CONTRACT

Thomas Hobbes changed the rules of the political game forever in 1651, when his great work of political philosophy was published. *Leviathan, or the Matter, Form and Power of a Commonwealth, Ecclesiastical and Civil* was the title of the book. It proposed a new theory of the state.

Hobbes's thinking places him firmly in the passage from Jean Bodin to John Locke. He denies Bodin's idea that the right to rule emanates from the communion between a human king and a divine being (God, let's say). Instead, he insists that it derives from a contract between a sovereign (who may in fact be a cabal of men) and a people. There is no divine right to rule. Instead there are civil rights to protection of life and property granted by a sovereign to a people once they have surrendered their natural right to warlike behaviour and proclaimed their obedience.

Once an individual breaks this social contract, he recovers his natural right to enmity and declares himself an outlaw. He may be arrested and killed by the state according to the rules of war. Usually, this killing has a ritual aspect. It is designed as a spectacle to remind people of the power of the sovereign and keep them in awe. As Hobbes says, "And Covenants, without the Sword, are but Words, and of no strength to secure a man at all."

The state executioner occupies a ceremonial office which partakes of sovereignty. The hangman is the hidden double of the ruler (whether king, queen or cabal). That is why he is hooded or masked. He is the ruler unknown to himself, an autonomous figure who escapes his own representation as the embodiment of the people.

10

26

His is the true face of naked power.

Natural rights are repressed in the thought of Locke, shuffled to the bottom of the deck when it comes to an understanding of the social contract. Locke amplifies, develops and secures the scope of individual civil rights, pushing them in the direction of a right to peace, a right to liberty, a right to the pursuit of happiness – and perhaps, some day soon, a right to celebrity. However, these are all mere substantive illusions when the origin of the state in revolutionary violence and the curbing of absolute freedom is forgotten.

Hobbes wrote *Leviathan* in the midst of civil war. He claims that people have a natural right to desert their sovereign if he fails to protect them. This is not opportunism. It is survivalism. Hobbes started out on one side in the English Civil War and ended up on the other side – the winning side - once it was all over.

Hobbes's theory depends upon a particular understanding of human nature. Men and women are like wild animals in their natural state. They are dangerous and much inclined to war. That is the measure of their innocence.

The radical sects of the English Civil War had a different view of human nature. The Church of Albion, for example, thought that the universe manifested itself in acts of love and cooperation between men and women. There was no need for a sovereign.

In the twentieth century, the problem of the state was most clearly articulated in the dispute between the Nazi political philosopher Carl Schmitt and the Jewish mystic Walter Benjamin. For Benjamin, the eruption of revolutionary violence against the state is legitimate because grounded in laws of universal brotherhood and sisterhood. Schmitt shares Hobbes's view that this is a dangerous illusion. However, whereas Hobbes grants the rebellious monarchist or sectarian anarchist his natural right to declare war, Schmitt insists that the sovereign can proclaim a state of emergency which trumps this right. The outlaw is brought under a sovereign rule which is now totalitarian. He has no rights at all. He is in fact barely human.

Schmitt goes to the root of Hobbes. For Hobbes, the social contract makes the sovereign the legal representative of the people. But sovereignty exceeds the claims of the people and is autonomous. Schmitt's move is theoretically possible. It defines a kind of divine right to rule without the divinity. Sovereignty is directly embodied in the person of the ruler, in their words and gestures, their looks and their personality.

It was Cromwell, with his outbursts and mood swings, his crazed hallucinations, who established the hysterical performance mode of all subsequent dictators. The sovereign is above the people, more than human, but cut off from God. He is a kind of demon conjured by the people in a ritual pact, where obedience is offered up in exchange for protection. He is an entity contracted to inhabit the body of a designated individual for a certain period of time.

Hobbes was not unaware of this dimension of the social contract. In *Leviathan*, he characterises heathen governance precisely as a species of demonology, in which pagans worshipped "the Dead... whom they Dreamed, were not inhabitants of their own Brain, but of the Air, or of Heaven, or Hell; not Phantasms, but Ghosts".

A human being possessed by the collective spirit of sovereignty becomes a kind of sacred victim. They are used up by the power of command, which manifests as charisma. Once spent, their remains are discarded. The act of ritual surrender can be savage. The body vacated by sovereignty is still

11

sacred, but is now impure. It has to be expelled from society. Cromwell was ritually executed after his death. By the time of the Restoration, he was the obvious scapegoat for a new capitalist class anxious to disavow its complicity in his crimes. His rotting corpse was disinterred from Westminster Abbey, dragged to Tyburn and hanged as a felon. Afterwards, it was cut down and decapitated. Cromwell's severed head was placed on a spike at Westminster Hall. Once the skin had fallen away, the skull became a profane token. It was taken down and passed between the curiosity cabinets of the wealthy.

Just as Hobbes is the vanishing mediator between Bodin and Locke, so Cromwell flashes briefly in the passage from the absolute monarchies of the Tudors and the Stuarts to the constitutional governments of the Whigs and the Tories. Both Hobbes and Cromwell have been repressed in historical memory. Their legacy is everywhere.

THE BEAST LEVIATHAN

It is said that unlike the United States of America, the United Kingdom lacks a written constitution. That is certainly true. The British constitution is instead encoded in an image.

It was Hobbes who designed this image. It adorns the title page of *Leviathan* as an engraving. It is an icon of the British state.

Shown is a colossus, a giant man, whose upper body rises from the land like a spirit of the earth. This body is composed of many tiny figures. They gaze up at the crowned head of the giant. From one perspective, they appear as the chains on his coat of mail. From another perspective, they are the scales on his serpent-like skin. Together they compose the man, but they are also his property.

12

The huge figure is Leviathan, an "artificial man" who both represents and rules over his people. He holds a sword in one hand and a crozier in the other, conventional symbols of civil and ecclesiastical power. The British sovereign is both Crown-in-Parliament and Supreme Governor of the state church. Jurisdiction is claimed over the souls as well as the bodies of men and women, and yet there is no claim made for access to divine power.

This is the image of a demon, or a "mortal god" as Hobbes characterised Leviathan. This was even more obvious in Hobbes's original sketch for the title page of his book, which saw the tiny figures with their faces turned outwards to the spectator and gave the overall impression of a crowned devil with many heads.

Hobbes glossed his image with a quote from the Book of Job

– "There is no power on earth to be compared to him." The dissident religious sects of the English Civil War also loved to quote from the Bible. It was how they preached the case for their own radical politics. It is as if Hobbes were here disputing with the anarchists on their own territory of prophecy and Hermetic magic, conjuring a demon from the pages of the Bible in order to terrorise them. It is perhaps one of the reasons why he gave this devil his own face.

In the Book of Job, Leviathan is a monster of the deep, a sea serpent, invested with Satanic attributes: "His scales are his pride, shut up together as with a close seal."

In English law there is an idea that the land is really owned by the sovereign alone. An individual owns not the land, but an estate in the land. This amounts to the right to use the land and exclude others from using it, a civil right granted by the sovereign, a right both transferable and inheritable.

Estates in the land are thus, according to Hobbes, like the scales of Leviathan. As the Book of Job says: "They are joined one to another, they stick together, that they cannot be sundered." What binds estates together and makes their owners peaceable are the property markers which separate them, the fences and hedges of the English countryside, including the drystone walls of the Peak District.

"A CATARACT OF BLOOD MIXED WITH FIRE"

William Blake was a poet much given to visions. When he was a child, playing on the common in South London, he saw an angel ablaze on a tree. In an earlier time, he would have been known as a prophet and a martyr of the radical Gnostic sects. As it was, Blake was a member of a surviving remnant of the Church of Albion, which, like the Quakers, was by the late eighteenth century a law-abiding shadow of its former glorious self.

In later life, Blake confined his visions to his poems. In *The Marriage of Heaven and Hell*, written in 1790 or so, he describes, in rather sardonic terms, an adult encounter with an angel. The angel takes the rebellious poet into a cave and together they travel deep underground. Blake hangs by the twisted roots of a tree over an abyss, where he sees not only the black sun of the alchemists, but devils flying through the air, and, there, rising from the void, the giant serpent Leviathan itself.

13

Like the shamans of old, Blake has temporarily relinquished his place in society and gone into the caves, where he is offered a vision of the underworld. He reclaims his natural right to freedom and confronts an image of the British state borrowed directly from Hobbes. This, says the angel as he flies away, is his "eternal lot."

But Blake disagrees. The vision changes from one of hell to one of heaven, as the poet sees no longer a serpent but someone playing a harp by the riverside. Blake returns above ground and challenges his angel, who is surprised to discover that he has escaped. The poet explains that he simply exercised the power of his imagination to change the picture with which he was presented.

Blake understands that heaven and hell are states of mind, not metaphysical realities. He further understands that the British state is a collective hallucination, engineered through habits of mind and patterns of behaviour. Leviathan is no demon. He is only a picture in a book.

The invisible insurrection of millions of minds, Blake suggests, is only ever one prophetic thought away.

AULT HUCKNALL

Ault Hucknall in the Peak District is said to be the smallest village in England. Its church is dedicated to St John the Baptist, a Christian prophet having affinities with certain water deities.

In the graveyard just beyond the porch, almost barring access, is a yew tree which is said to be 4,000 years old. Some people once believed it was rooted in the underworld.

The pagan associations of this place of worship do not end there. The church walls inside are studded with weird stone devices, little grinning faces sculpted in the shape of leaves, remnants of the local cult of the Green Man. Branches and vines sprout from the nose, the mouth of the Green Man, bearing fruit and flowers. Once, people would have made offerings to this deity, to ensure they were blessed with good crops. The Green

14

Man was a fertility god attended to by Druidic priests decked in mistletoe. He demanded human sacrifice.

Thomas Hobbes was carried to this church after his death. The funeral procession moved along one of the many corpse roads which mark the Peak, those old straight tracks which pass under the drystone walls, and which many imagine are the songlines or dreaming paths of the old shamans.

A black marble slab inscribed with Hobbes's name was laid in the south aisle, though nobody knows for sure where the man himself is buried.

WATCHTOWER

On a steep hill in the Peak District there lie the ruined stones of Hardwick Old Hall. The place is roofless and exposed, its ground floor overgrown with grass, its walls gaping with massive rectangular holes which once were filled with glass.

The west wing overlooks the distant motorway. It is a shambles of crumbling stairways, collapsed floors and trembling walls supported by scaffolding. On the fourth floor, at the top of the section, is a room known as the Giants Chamber. It was once the great hall where the Cavendish family held public ceremonies and entertained their guests. The plasterwork over the fireplace still survives.

Hardwick Old Hall was commissioned as a princely residence by Bess of Hardwick, Elizabethan matriarch of the Cavendish family, in 1591. Only six years later, in a mania of conspicuous consumption, fuelled by crazed dreams of ruling the kingdom, this prodigious woman constructed the even grander Hardwick Hall, just next door. The new place became notorious for its gaudy windows, which were given added sparkle by locally mined lead.

Hardwick Old Hall was abandoned by Bess and left to become the service block for her new country house. It was inhabited by guests and servants and it was here that Hobbes came to live when he was employed as a tutor to the household. His place of study was the Giants Chamber.

Hobbes set up his telescope next to the open window and sat at his desk with his books. The huge fireplace was filled with burning coals. And, there, at each side of the mantelpiece, set

15

in the wall, were two painted plasterwork effigies, one of Gog and the other of Magog. The twin giants of Ancient Britain, aboriginals of the land, stared down at Hobbes with closely lidded eyes.

Hobbes was grappling with the problems of mechanics. Suspended in the time of passage from John Dee to Isaac Newton, from magic to science, he was attempting to banish the supercelestial aspect of mechanics, that part of it dealing with the bodies of angels and the occult forces of attraction between the moon and stars. He wrote in Latin. The manuscripts piled up, as did the plans for various great works attempting to synthesize the modern scientific thinking of the day.

Hobbes never succeeded in writing an equivalent to *Leviathan* in the field of mechanics, a work to banish the lingering traces of magic and prepare the way for a properly atheistic scientific conception of the world. Nobody did. Newton was later able to unify the theories of Kepler and Galileo with his three laws of motion, but his idea of gravity, with its emphasis on action at a distance, still retained traces of supercelestial mechanics. Hobbes had not done the work to prevent Newton from remaining a closet alchemist, conducting late-night experiments with metals suspended in nitrate solution, which he saw coming to life and growing like plants.

Compare Newton with Locke. It was precisely because Hobbes had made a clean break with superstition in the field of political philosophy, that Locke was able to develop his model of civil rights without being bothered by any lingering traces of a revealed God.

There was a partial failure of world historical imagination in the early seventeenth century. The delivery of the modern universe from the medieval cosmos was botched. Hobbes in his Giants Chamber is the guilty demiurge. He was not able to create a unified theory of everything.

Outside Hardwick, on the rutted paths of the Peak District,

travelled the cunning men, with their Tarot cards and almanacs, their various systems of prophecy. They would pitch up tent in a village and tell people's fortunes. They have never really gone away.

HE TRAVELLED TO SEVEN DIFFERENT PLACES

It was 1626 and Thomas Hobbes was coming to the end of his first stint of employment for the Cavendish family. He was aware that the young man he had been tutoring would one day inherit the title to the family's estates in the Peak District. Hobbes wanted to give the impressionable aristocrat something to remember him by, a distinctive mark of his learning, a demonstration of his scholarly credentials. The result was a poem.

Hobbes composed *De Mirabilibus Pecci* in Latin hexameters and formally dedicated the five hundred or so lines to his young charge. He offered him the poem on New Year's Day and received the sum of £5 in return. In 1636, the poem was translated as *The Wonders of the Peak*.

Hobbes's literary effort belongs to the genre of the estate poem, which had been used by ambitious poets to secure patronage from landed aristocrats ever since Ben Jonson wrote *To Penhurst* for Sir Robert Sidney in 1616. *The Wonders of the Peak*, for all its classical Greek allusion, is effectively an inventory of Cavendish real estate in the East Midlands of England.

16

The poem describes a journey over the course of a day. Hobbes saddles up and rides out with a tour party to view seven fabled wonders of the Peak. They are conducted on their way by various unnamed guides. Hobbes includes local folklore and some reportage amidst his effusions. He does not specify the villages he passes through, judging their names too vulgar for his Latin tongue.

FIRST STOP ON THE TOUR

The chief residence of the Cavendish family in the Peak District has always been Chatsworth House. It was originally bought in 1549 for £600 by Sir Charles Cavendish, who was husband to Bess of Hardwick, and it is still occupied by his descendants today. The family has certainly had other places to live in the Peak, such as Hardwick Hall, but Chatsworth has been their main address.

The history of Chatsworth is a history of the redesign of surrounding lands, the transformation of habitat into spectacle. One of the Cavendish line demolished a hill which blocked his sight of a valley, while another relocated an entire village in order to improve his view. Even the course of the River Derwent was altered in these various terra-forming exercises.

Hobbes devotes many lines of his poem to singing the praises of Chatsworth House and it is the place where his journey begins.

During the English Civil War, when Hobbes was in exile, the Peak District was under the sway of Cromwell's military forces. Sir John Gell was a prominent local capitalist whose sheep farming enterprises had benefited from the enclosure of common lands. He came out for the revolutionary party at the start of the war, raised bands of cavalry and infantry and garrisoned his troops at Derby. In 1643, he was made military commander of three counties in the English Midlands.

The Cavendish family, like most aristocratic landowners in the Peak, were on the side of the king in the Civil War. This created an uneasy political situation where houses like Chatsworth and Hardwick acted as monarchist strongholds in an area which was nominally under revolutionary control. The grandees of the revolutionary army frequently called upon Gell to push south from his base to combat monarchist forces. This he did. However, his troops were more interested in the plunder to be gained from sacking the great houses of the Peak.

The cavalry regiments were full of men of independent thought. They were reading the Hermetic texts of philosophy, newly translated from the Latin, and mixing with the religious sectarians in the lower ranks. There was much talk of the looting of treasure, the sharing of resources, the building of an egalitarian commonwealth. Chatsworth and Hardwick were widely seen as the storehouses of a confiscated social energy.

The dream was to ride into Chatsworth, stable the horses in the great hall, where they would soil the rich carpets, and take down the paintings of the Cavendish line. Everything would be thrown on a bonfire, including the mortgage deeds to local properties and other contracts of law. There would be dancing to the music of the pipe and the drum, a festival of destruction, the cancelling of all debts and the chance for everyone to start again from zero.

17

The Church of Albion stated that the dead would be summoned from the underworld and the angels called down from heaven. God himself would join in the celebrations.

When these fantasies of destruction reached Cromwell and his advisers in London, they despatched a letter to the revolutionary committee in Derby. Gell was instructed that under no circumstances should Chatsworth House or Hardwick Hall be pulled down. It was 1645. The end of the Civil War was in sight. The army grandees were anxious to reach a new political settlement and perhaps grab some of these big houses for themselves.

Soon after the Second World War, when an armed population was rapidly demobilised, the Cavendish family found itself unable to pay death duties on its various properties in the Peak. Hardwick Hall was surrendered to a new reforming welfare state. Chatsworth House opened its doors to the paying public and set up a gift-shop in the grounds.

COUNTRY PILE

Hidden on top of one of the highest hills in England is a testing range owned by the British state. The perimeter of this Peak District site is fenced with wire. The interior is scored with public footpaths and policed by security guards. The place is one mile square. Here, there are many laboratories, there are trials areas for explosions and inter-linking roads. The grassy edges of the site are populated with sheep. Recently planted pine trees shield the zone from public view.

The place used to be a military site, where mortars were fired and munitions tested. Now it is occupied by the Health and Safety Laboratory.

The lab does not appear on any maps. Harpur Hill is certainly marked, just south of the spa town of Buxton. It is indicated that the approach road is lined with ex-local authority housing and the lower slopes of the hill are occupied by industrial estates. At the summit of the hill, the map shows the road fading away into a mysterious blank patch.

The reality on the ground is that there is a gatehouse at the end of the road, a security check, and entrance into the grounds of the lab. Crouched over the car-park is the main building, an edifice of black glass built into the side of the hill. It was constructed in 2005 and its flanks are clad in the same fossil limestone used in the local drystone walls. Orbiting the building is a ring-road, where the speed limit is 20 miles per hour.

When there is testing in the grounds, the red flag flies and the wail of a siren lifts above the noise of the wind.

This is a Category 3 lab, ranking one level below the highest security clearance in the kingdom. It is the place where industrial accidents are investigated. These accidents tend to be large-scale and may involve many deaths. They include rail crashes, crowd crushes, bridge collapses, tunnel fires and explosions in stores or warehouses. The lab's scientists are mobilised when the causes of an accident are not known or when there is grounds for suspicion of malpractice and a criminal prosecution might result. They conduct two to three hundred investigations every year and work for the police or for the Health and Safety Executive, a policy-making branch of the state.

The lab also conducts speculative work, both for its executive branch and for insurance companies.

The lab is guided in its work by the Health and Safety at Work Act. This became law in 1974, at the highest reforming moment of the welfare state. It is designed to protect the lives of people in public as they go about their lawful business.

There is a loop-hole in the law. Companies and other authorities are not required to carry out specified safety checks in the workplace. Instead, they are free to decide for themselves what inspections to make, based on what is "reasonably practicable". They are expected to make a calculation which racks up costs against benefits. There are potentially wasteful costs to be incurred spending time on unnecessary inspections. But there are benefits to be gained from avoiding the prosecutions and compensation claims resulting from death or injury.

Most often, the definition of what is "reasonably practicable" for a specific situation is only ever decided after an accident has occurred and there is a dispute over its causes. That is to say, it is decided in a criminal court. Under this circumstance, it is the scientific evidence presented by the accident investigators of the Health and Safety Laboratory which is critical in helping a jury to make up its mind and seal the outcome of a case.

The people of the United Kingdom all agree that science offers a certain path to the truth of an event. Even if they no longer share the same religious views and cannot accommodate themselves to a hegemonic Church of England, they still acknowledge the scientific legacy of the Royal Society.

When someone has died in an accident and the case is

brought to court, then it is the accident investigators who discover what caused the accident and who is to blame for the death. It is their testimony which determines whether the dead person's estate should receive a payment in compensation.

There is a rough consensus about the sum of money which should be paid in compensation for someone's death in an accident. It's about £4 million to £10 million. This figure is therefore the maximum amount which a company or other authority might be expected to spend on safety checks in order to save a life. Anything spent in excess of this figure is obviously not "reasonably practicable". This is something accepted by the investigators of the Health and Safety Laboratory. It is also, by implication, something accepted by the people of the United Kingdom when they choose to believe the scientific evidence presented by these investigators.

There is in effect a collective agreement about when it is right to sacrifice a human life. This social contract exists between the people and the state. It is a manifestation of the sovereignty of the state.

Now that capital punishment has been abolished and outlaws are no longer put to death by the state, now that the civil powers of sovereignty over life and death are increasingly repressed and invisibilised, it is difficult to discover contemporary embodiments of Hobbes's Leviathan in all its historic terror.

The accident investigators of the Health and Safety Laboratory, hidden away on an inaccessible hill in one of the remotest parts of England, working in a secure environment, offer one glimpse into the machinations of Leviathan. They fulfil a similar office to that of the state executioner, existing both within and on the other side of the law, marking the threshold between what is safe and unsafe, establishing the conditions for the despatch of designated victims to their fate.

SECOND TOUR LOCATION

Peak Cavern is the second of the seven wonders of the Peak described by Hobbes in his estate poem. It is still a tourist attraction today. It is located in the Castleton area, alongside Speedwell Cavern, Blue John Cavern and Treak Cliff Cavern.

Peak Cavern is the largest natural cave in Britain and has been regularly squatted by communities of travelling artisans. It was an annual gathering place for gypsies, where news was exchanged between continents and distant families reunited. It was also a holy place for the Church of Albion, back when it was called "the Devil's Arse".

Castleton used to be known as a mining district. Mineral-rich liquids had forced their way through cracks in the limestone of the Peak, millions of years ago, when the planet was settling itself. The lead ore, the copper ore and the fluorspar (known locally as "Blue John") ran in veins through the land for many miles. These "rakes" were deep and narrow.

Hobbes describes the work of the lead miners of Castleton in his poem. The men dug deep into the earth and followed the progress of the ore by tunnelling horizontally through the limestone. Shafts were sunk at regular intervals, their grassy remains still visible today at places such as Speedwell, Packthread, Hazard, Old Moor, Portway, Longcliffe, Old Tor and Odin.

Mining has always been a dangerous activity. Hobbes describes the scene of a mining accident in his poem. Two men have been killed as a result of what appears to be a collapsed mineshaft. The corpse of one

18

has been recovered for the funeral rites of the Church of England. The other body is still being searched for. A crowd has gathered to bear witness and for a moment, Hobbes is with them, looking down from his horse at the wailing women and troubled children. Then, a switch of the reins, and he and his party ride on.

There are over 20,000 abandoned mines in the Peak District. Once, the pigs of lead were exported across the western Roman Empire. There was another peak of production in Hobbes's time, during the seventeenth century and also the eighteenth century, when the metal was shipped out from Hull by the English East India Company. By the 1930s, however, the lead mines were exhausted. The last big mine closed in 1940.

The lead miners always saw themselves as a class apart from the rest of the Peak District. Their affairs were subject to a body of laws separate from the state, dating back in their oral form to a time centuries before the Norman Conquest and only incorporated into English law during the mid-nineteenth century. These laws were administered by the Barmote Court.

The two mining deaths witnessed by Hobbes would have been subject to an inquest conducted by the Barmote Court. This court also had the right to grant a lease to anyone who discovered a productive lead mine. It was almost as if the lead miners together formed their own sovereign body, one to rival that of the state, a petty Leviathan.

The laws governing the discovery, ownership and use of a lead mine in Hobbes's time were strange, like remnants from a deeper, older, vaster struggle. Any individual in search of a lead mine had the right to freely wander the lands of the Peak in the name of their real owner, who was thought to be the king (or queen). The estates leased to landowners by the sovereign included a right to use the surface of the land but there was no exclusive right to use what lay beneath. This was a right whose major part was reserved for miners.

A miner in his quest for lead had the right to jump the drystone walls which separated estates in the Peak. He could begin to dig anywhere, except in the public highway, which was the exclusive property of the sovereign. Once he found a vein of lead, its total value was estimated by the Barmote Court. The landowner had a right to a third of this sum. The remainder was claimed by the miner.

Often, a mine could be worked by one or two men, who might expect to earn a substantial living. As a result, they might also well consider themselves kings of the underworld.

The laws of the Barmote Court feel as if they were the conclusion of a peace settlement reached long ago in ancient times by two sovereign bodies. There was perhaps the king of the land, who possessed a special relationship with the god of the sky, in an early form of the divine right to rule. And then there was the king of the underworld, who claimed jurisdiction over all those who lived and worked underground, including, perhaps, the souls of the dead.

Is this too fanciful? It was what the Church of Albion believed. And it certainly explains why the lead miners of the Peak followed the regiments of King Charles in the English Civil War. They preferred the partial sovereignty granted them by a distant king to the subsistence tenancy on offer from an improving capitalist landowner.

The lead miners of the Peak District had their own collective body of folklore. They believed in the existence of spirits who inhabited the tunnels where they worked. These ghosts had the power to guide them. The miners called them Tommyknockers.

The Tommyknockers were very rarely seen. Instead, they

19

were most often heard. Underground messengers, they communicated through noise and vibration, the propagation of low-frequency sound. The miners would tap out a call on the walls of the tunnels, their hammers drumming on the rock. The response would not be long in coming. It was a matter of locating echoes from distant passageways, catching a rhythm, inventing a code.

The miners told each other stories. A lightly pulsed, trebly pattern of echoes meant there was a rich mineral vein ahead. A single, low note announced that a roof-fall was imminent. Whistling was strictly taboo. The Tommyknockers were said to be offended by high-frequency noises. The short soundwaves were instantly sucked up by the holes in the limestone. No echo could ever occur. There was never a response to the call.

The more superstitious miners appeased the Tommy-knockers with offerings of food and tallow. The spirits were unpredictable and capricious. They could lead miners astray, trapping them underground in a limbo state of endless wandering, claiming them eventually as one of their own.

The shamans of the Upper Paleolithic era would have understood the Tommyknockers. They were spirits of the dead, voices of the ancestors, messengers of the gods. They were to be contacted through the ritual use of sound, through low-frequency drumming, chanting and the humming of bullroarers as they were whirled over the head. The shamans would use the acoustic properties of the caves, the resonances and echoes, to induce trance. Once in this state, they would commune with the spirits, reaching out beyond the buzzing limestone network of caves and tunnels to connect with the gods beyond.

This attachment to an idea of the freedom which lies underground is something shared by all miners. Certainly, the miners who worked in the coal fields which surrounded the Peak District, especially in the east, around Sheffield, possessed a fierce sense of their own sovereignty. They were not afraid to challenge their overseers by exercising a counter-strategy of strikes and industrial sabotage. There were memorable clashes between the miners and the forces of the state many times in the twentieth century – in 1926, 1972, 1974 and 1984. On occasion, the government declared a state of emergency. Very often, these events had the colour of war.

GREAT HALL

The Health and Safety Laboratory outside Buxton dramatises and makes visible the sovereign powers of the state. It is as if Hobbes's Leviathan rears up its giant body from the grounds of Harpur Hill and, safely shielded from public gaze, exercises its powers of command.

When the lab is called upon to investigate an accident, it has the right to take possession of the debris. Its officers will arrive at the scene of an accident, document it, and secure the evidence. This evidence might comprise the twisted tracks and train carriages of a rail disaster, the buckled steel supports of a collapsed bridge, the charred remains of a warehouse fire. Whatever it might be, the material is loaded up and taken to Harpur Hill.

The trail of evidence linking the debris to the original accident site is preserved at all times. State officers keep the material within line of sight if it is being transported on the roads by a third party.

All accident debris is stored in the evidence hangar on Harpur Hill. This unobtrusive, grey warehouse is one of the support structures which service the lab's main stone-clad building. The contents of the evidence hangar are subject to a legal taboo. They cannot be publicly reported.

Items variously stashed in the evidence hangar in the past include sections of rail track, crushed train carriages, a lift with a brass cage, exploded pipes from a water main, various nuts and bolts, a fairground ride car, a tower crane and part of a nuclear submarine.

Inside the lab's main building, towards the back, is the place where accident debris is brought from the hangar for testing and analysis. This is the incident lab.

The incident lab is a cavernous space with hidden possibilities for complete control. There is a movable gantry set into the ceiling from which test materials can be suspended. The removable steel slats slotted in the floor make it simple for materials to be pinioned. Between the graspable architecture of ceiling and floor lies a strategic volume of fluid three-dimensional space.

Space and force are vectors which the lab's accident investigators need to control. Their experiments depend upon Newton's laws of motion. Control over the equally significant dimension of time is supplied by the lab's high-speed video cameras, which capture movement at fractions of a millisecond.

This coefficient of control turns the incident lab into a real-life simulation chamber, a studio within which reality effects are repeatedly manufactured for analysis. Not only can stressed or broken components from an accident be studied in their impure state, but fresh and unsullied copies of these same components can be manipulated in space and time to see how they perform under pressure. Comparison between the original debris from the accident and the debris recently manufactured in the lab always yields much insight.

The whole point about an accident is that it is what the French theorist Paul Virilio calls an "unknown quantity". When an accident occurs, nobody knows what has happened. All that is known is that what should have happened, didn't happen. Something else happened instead. Often, this results in a disturbance of the official record, a voiding of the semi-automatic archiving processes which record and transcribe events. It is the task of the accident investigators to discover the cause of the accident and banish the quantity that is unknown. Their method is to recreate the accident in the controlled conditions of the incident lab.

How is this simulation accomplished? Fist, the investigators identify the events leading up to the accident and the events following on from the accident. Then, they plot the events on a timeline in order to identify the sequencing of the accident, the unknown quantity which must have existed in the interval between the "before" and the "after" of the accident. This is a gap in consensus reality. It is a hole in the archive of the state.

Next, the investigators conjure a plausible scenario to explain the accident and model it using Newton's laws of motion. This is done through application of the equations of classical mechanics or, in more complex cases, the use of computational fluid dynamics. Finally, the scenario is enacted in real time and space using physical copies of the accident materials. More than one scenario might need to be tested before an exact match with the evidence and the known course of events is achieved.

In this way, for example, the root cause of a train derailment involving many deaths might be traced to a loose nut on the line. It is then a matter of deciding in court who is responsible for the loose nut. Once a legal settlement is reached, then an explanation of the train derailment has been collectively agreed upon. The gap in reality created by the accident has been bridged, the hole in the archive has been filled.

One of the things at stake here is the social frame of the science of classical mechanics. Newton's laws of motion dictate the course of an event in a pure space – such as the mathematical field of a computer simulation or the controlled three-dimensional space of an incident lab. However, once the science of mechanics is applied to a socially constructed space – such as a workplace or a public transport facility – then it becomes the discipline of mechanical engineering. It is subject to many impure admixtures, including the results of risk assessment around safety.

The safety recommendations issued by the Health and Safety Lab go on to affect the social framing of mechanical engineering. They function as a collective judgement on the number of human injuries and deaths which can be accepted before a structure is declared to be unsafe or not likely to endure.

Narrative is one of the other major outputs of the lab's accident investigators. Their reports and expert witness presentations tell the story of what happened during an accident for the period that reality was suspended. Their papers, files, photos and videos are grafted on to the wound in the official record created by the accident and its disturbance of received memory. The lab's records are the necessary supplement to the state archive.

20

In sum, the Health and Safety Lab is a kind of switching station which imports evidence from the site of an accident and exports documentation to fill the gap in the official record. The lab's accident investigation reports compensate for the failure of consensus reality triggered by the accident. They reboot the archive.

The lab performs a kind of alchemical miracle. It retrieves the sullen rubble of the material world from beneath the fissures in the archive, makes use of them in the imitation of an action and transforms them into agreeable signs. The archive is patched up with its own excreta. The reality principle is saved through intervention of a simulation.

The simulation has always been known since ancient times as a copy without an original. Here, the simulation stands in for an original which has gone missing, like a phantom limb which is treated as if it were real.

Once a case is closed by the lab's investigators, the accident debris loses its status as evidence and becomes merely property. The original owners are free to

21

recover the items, but many do not, seeing them as generators of bad publicity. These unlucky objects are perhaps, in the popular mind, imagined to be so many guilty nuts and bolts. It is no wonder these items find it so extremely difficult to re-enter society. Sometimes, they are sold for scrap. Most often, they are transported to the lab's workshops and either chopped into little pieces or burned. They are effectively put beyond use.

GOGMAGOG

According to the official chroniclers, Gogmagog was one of the aboriginal giants who lived in Britain when it was still known as Albion, long before the emergence of the state.

These giants were naturally destructive and spent their time fighting each other in festivals of war. Gogmagog was the last of them. He was defeated in combat by the first king of Britain and thrown off a cliff into the sea.

This tale is told in the twelfth century by Geoffrey of Monmouth to justify the Norman Conquest and again in the seventeenth century by John Milton when the state was reorganized by Oliver Cromwell.

In some versions of the story, Gogmagog is in fact a pair of twins, Gog and Magog. These brothers spend their time combating each other if they have no common enemy to occupy them.

22

The Church of Albion worships Gogmagog as an ancestor god. The deity presides over all those who are exiles in their own land – the Saxons crushed by the Normans, the religious dissidents, political radicals and fanatical monarchists suppressed by Cromwell, miners crushed by the state, the wanderers and prophets of all times.

It is said that the exiled giant lives on in the caves of the British Isles, where his sighs and moans can still be heard.

"ROSES ARE PLANTED WHERE THORNS GROW"

In the poem *The Marriage of Heaven and Hell*, William Blake sets out his argument in the first few lines. He says the "perilous

23

path" is originally occupied by the "just man", who is witness to divine miracles such as springs flowing in the desert. This attracts the notice of the envious "villain" from the "paths of ease", who moves into the territory scouted by the just man and drives him out into the "wilds" and the "barren heath".

This is an allegory of the displacement of tribes and populations. The shamans and prophets are displaced by the priests of organized religion, the Church of Albion is displaced by the Church of England, the people of Gogmagog are displaced by the agents of the state.

Blake goes on to say how the just man in exile is accompanied by Rintrah, the god of righteous anger, holy war and jihad.

It is clear that Rintrah is another name for Gogmagog.

HUNTING LODGE

The Health and Safety Laboratory has many testing ranges in the wilderness tended by its janitors. The fire and explosion trials area is where work is done into accidents involving explosives, flammable liquids and hydrogen gas. The blackened fire engulfment pit and concrete test pads are monitored by cameras and subject to an exclusion zone.

A short distance away are the control buildings which receive the audio-video feed from the trials area. They are two squat cottages built from drystone. The doors are made of reinforced steel, the windows are armoured with hinged steel shutters. They look as if they have been made to survive a terrorist attack.

Next to one of the control buildings is a radio tower.

A red rag flies from the flag-pole when explosion trials are conducted.

THIRD STOP

The third of the seven wonders of the Peak visited by Hobbes in his poem is Mam Tor. This ancient conical hill rises between two valleys, just to the west of Castleton. It is known as the "shivering mountain", because layers of exposed gritstone and shale constantly break up and slide down its sides.

Legend has it that although the hill is constantly eroding, it casts the same sized shadow, as if preserved by some mysterious force.

The hills of the Peak District were once marked with the gallows, whose sinister cross-beams were silhouetted on the

 skyline for many miles around. Here is where outlaws were hanged by the authorities, in full view of the surrounding population, as a fatal reminder of the power of the state. The gallows is an engine of Hobbesian sovereignty, one of the favoured weapons of Leviathan.

The idea was that the sight of the hanged man would make people think twice before reclaiming their natural right to make war on the state. It was an act of terror.

24

There have been many inclined to become outlaws in the history of the Peak. The discarded remnants of the English Civil War hid themselves in the district's wild places and, refusing to compromise with the new composition of the state, made a living as bandits.

Defeated monarchist officers, bereft of their estates, which had been sequestered, turned to highway robbery. They held up coaches at gunpoint and robbed the occupants.

Of much lower caste were the footpads who had quit the New Model Army in disgust, when their wages were not paid and they did not receive the New Jerusalem they were promised. These bitter and vengeful men used long staves to attack commercial travellers on the trade routes between Nottingham and Matlock Spa. They stole their money. They threw their bodies down the potholes and mine shafts.

In the eighteenth century, these renegades were joined by peasants dispossessed of their livelihoods by the enclosure of the common lands.

The bandits were often part of a larger black economy. Innkeepers would advise them of the movements of travelling merchants, shopkeepers would fence stolen goods for them, others would inform them of shipments of goods that were due. The riches stolen by bandits trickled back into the local community in the form of bribes and corrupt fees.

It is no surprise that these figures, especially the highwaymen, with their lordly ways, were mythologized by local people as champions of the redistribution of wealth. For agricultural labourers and estate employees, with their lives of perpetual servitude, the highwayman, with his natural freedom of the Peak, symbolised their dreams of a world liberated from exploitation and oppression.

25

For the authorities, of course, the highwayman remained a criminal. One of the tasks of the state was to counter the lasting impression left on people's minds by the heroic image of the highwayman. The body of the hanged felon was in that sense still a useful property. Left to rot in an iron cage suspended by chains from a hilltop, it worked as a propaganda tool, reminding those who passed on the road below of the power of Leviathan over outlaws.

The body of the dead man was coated in tar to preserve him against the elements. That way, he would endure longer as a spectacle. The chains of the gibbet clanked in the wind, the iron plates creaked and groaned. Here was an example of state violence impossible to ignore. It is no wonder that those sympathetic to the dead hero, his friends and allies, would set the man's tarred corpse on fire to liberate his memory. The flames leapt into the night for many miles around.

It is said that Dick Turpin was a highwayman in the Peak. His name features among the saints of the Church of Albion.

"GOGMAGOG ROARS AND SHAKES HIS FIRES"

Gogmagog is a god of righteous war called Rintrah in the poem *The Marriage of Heaven and Hell* by William Blake. Rintrah also features heavily in Blake's poem, *Europe*. This is a prophecy of the eruption in Britain of the kind of popular justice contained in the French Revolution of 1789. Blake envisages this surge of moral outrage displacing the old order of things in a flux of violence.

Rintrah, god of smoke and fire, is invoked in *Europe* by a sky-goddess. Here, the prospective marriage of heaven and hell announces an English Revolution which is so pervasive it feels like an apocalypse. Blake captures this mood in the illustrated plate on which is engraved his invocation – "Arise O Rintrah... O lion Rintrah raise thy fury from thy forests black." There is a red glow reflected in the dark clouds which billow and mass in the background. In the foreground, stands an old man with a vulnerable young woman clinging pitifully to his waist. He extends his arms with palms raised upwards, as if warding off some terrible danger of which the red glow is only a signal. His trailing white hair and long grey beard combined with his blue gown signify that he is a member of Britain's ruling elite, always given a perverse Druidic styling by Blake.

26

The engraved image is the perfect emblem of Leviathan warding off the anticipated violence of Gogmagog (an action which in the history of Blake's own time, and much to his disappointment, was entirely successful).

IMITATING THE EVENT HE FEARS

The very first accidents investigated by the Health and Safety Laboratory were coal mining accidents. The accidents originally simulated by their investigators were tunnel explosions, coal truck rail crashes and bucket elevator drops at the pithead. The sovereignty so often fiercely contested between miners and officers of the state in the streets and fields of Britain was something which could be safely explored and tested in the defensible space of Harpur Hill.

At the start of the twentieth century, the coal mining industry in Britain was at its peak. It employed over one million men. The work was dangerous. One thousand men died every year, half of them from falls of ground, many others from explosions. Firedamp and coal dust were most often the causes of these explosions, which could kill one hundred or so men in a single disaster.

The miners first organised into a nationwide union in 1889, with the formation of the Miners' Federation of Great Britain. The union fought for better working conditions for over 20 years and finally compelled the state to introduce the Mines Regulation Act in 1911. The Home Office Experimental Station was established in the same year and much of its early work was dedicated to testing the initially controversial theory that coal dust was explosive. In 1927, the station moved to Harpur Hill, safely out of range of the pit villages, so that now its noisy testing could be camouflaged by explosions from the nearby stone quarries.

The legacy of this activity survives to the present day in the grounds of Harpur Hill, where the old mines safety test equipment is tended by the state's mechanical engineers. The lab has a legal responsibility to maintain the rigs and keep them operational, even though they are technically obsolete because of the decline of the coal mining industry.

A slow drive across the contoured terrain of Harpur Hill reveals the resting places of these safety rigs. There is the replica of an underground roadway, a facsimile of a coal mining tunnel driven into barren limestone rock, now used for setting fire to things like fridges to test their flammability. There is a narrow gauge rail track, complete with control buildings instead of a station, once used to carry scale model coal trucks and test the impact of their collisions. There is also a drop test rig, comprising an iron hoisting arm attached to a tower, once used to determine the weight at which an elevator's cables might snap at the pithead.

A large white concrete pipe runs the length of the central grounds for hundreds of yards like an exposed artery of the underworld. Raised on the grassy earthworks of an obsolete railway and higher by far than a man, this large overground tunnel is capped at one end by a heavy blast door of two-foot thick concrete. The lab's investigators conducted their first experiments into coal mining explosions with this device.

The various safety rigs bring to the surface and expose the otherwise inaccessible working habitat of the miners. The overground tunnel, for example, takes the hole dug into the earth and pulls its lining inside-out to make a kind of exhibit of the underworld.

These rigs were used by the state to simulate the native domain of a rival sovereign body, that of the miners. The expressed aim of these reconstructions was to understand the causes of mining accidents and improve working conditions. The unconscious drive was to control the unstable space of a potential adversary by repeating it and reworking it in a safe environment, rehearsing the shape of a possible counter-insurgency strategy.

The grounds of the Health and Safety Laboratory on Harpur Hill are where the underground roadways of the miners are extracted and folded into the surveillance fields of the state, where underworld echoes and whispers meet ethereal radio waves, where the giant of the earth, Gogmagog, is laid out for the inspection of Leviathan in a rehearsal of some finally explosive cosmic marriage between heaven and hell.

TO STAVE OFF THE REAL EVENT

The founding principle of accident investigation at the Health and Safety Laboratory is imitation. Only when the unknown event is replicated for the first time can it be known and mastered. Accidents can be simulated on a computer using modelling software. However, the courts prefer to see evidence of a live simulation conducted in the material world. It's more difficult to argue against this.

The components of an accident simulation are designed and built in the workshops of the lab. Carpenters and joiners labour to construct scale models of many different landscapes, machines and structures from wood, metal and plastic. They work from photographs of the accident sites, maps, investigator field notes and surveyors' reports.

The craftsmen at the lab have built a one-third scale model of the London Underground escalator and booking hall at King's Cross station. They have also built models of the Hillsborough football stadium, the Buncefield oil storage depot, rail tracks and train carriages from Ladbroke Grove station and the Channel Tunnel, and various items of industrial plant.

Once the lab's investigators have discovered the causes of an accident, they go on to make recommendations intended to reduce the likelihood of the accident happening again. These recommendations can include changes in materials, components, tasks, processes or behaviours.

Similar recommendations also emerge from tests run on equipment which has not yet been involved in an accident but which the lab's investigators think it's advisable to test for safety flaws. They might well take a new kind of crane, or a new kind of platform lift, and subject it to stresses and loads in order to determine the nature and location of any fracture points. Here, accidents are deliberately conjured from materials in order to be better understood.

There is a preemptive as well as a reactive type of accident investigation. In both cases, the intention is the same. Accidents are simulated under controlled laboratory conditions, in a safe and sequestered space, in order to prevent them from happening in the far distant places of the real world outside of Harpur Hill.

It is as if the discipline of mechanical engineering, finding itself threatened by an unknown quantity it cannot explain, shucks off its applied social dimension and retreats to the pure space of classical mechanics, where it obsessively rehearses its founding equations until it recovers from shock. There seems to be a ritual element to this repetition compulsion.

Is it too much to imagine that accident investigation, with its focus on imitation and action at a distance, has affinities with the principles of sympathetic magic or voodoo?

27

There is certainly a difference of intention. The event imitated is something which is feared rather than something which is desired, something to be averted rather than something to be embraced, an event which is blocked and not channelled.

However, there remains a shared understanding that an imitation is effective because it is magically compelling. In voodoo, the imitation creates a symbolic debt which is paid for with the real event. In accident investigation, there is more of a short-circuit as the imitation attempts to double up as both debt and repayment. In both cases, there is an appeal to a supercelestial force which governs the eternal circulation of atoms. (This force might well be experienced by a shaman as a near-death experience.)

The reactive kind of accident investigation has implicit affinities with voodoo. When the lab's investigators build a scale model of the site of an accident, using debris from the scene to guide them, they are close in spirit to the shaman who makes a voodoo doll of his victim, using their hair, nail clippings and other leavings as part of the constituents. The lab's investigators create an effigy of the accident site – whether it's a bridge or a tunnel or a station platform – and then they do the scientific equivalent of sticking pins in it. They destroy it – by blowing it up or setting fire to it – under controlled conditions.

With the preemptive kind of accident investigation, which tests equipment and materials to breaking point, the short-circuiting of imitation and real event is more obvious. Fridges are set on fire in tunnels, lifts are run continuously over months, until the cables snap. Train carriages are blown up. This kind of action blurs the boundaries between the symbolic and the real in an unconscious sleight of hand. It is a god trick.

There were philosophers living and working in the time of Thomas Hobbes, cunning men popular with the Church of Albion, who would have characterised this bargaining with death as a demonic pact. Furthermore, they would have understood that a demon is simply a symbolic organisation of those supercelestial forces which pervade the universe and conduct actions between bodies. This animistic understanding of mechanics was what Hobbes worked hard to negate in his lifetime. He was unsuccessful. Only Isaac Newton in the late seventeenth century seemed to have the power to banish magic and create the platform for a properly material and atheistic conception of mechanics.

However, it may be that Newton arrived too late to do a thorough job. The science of classical mechanics explains the behaviour of natural or manmade bodies such as bridges and trains. It also explains the behaviour of celestial bodies such as planets and stars. What it does not explain is the behaviour of atomic particles in the supercelestial universe. Required for this is the science of quantum mechanics.

The occult mechanics of pre-scientific times was able to explain the natural, the celestial and the supercelestial worlds. It offered a unified theory of everything. However, classical mechanics and quantum mechanics are incompatible systems. The early twentieth century scientist Niels Bohr tried to patch things up when he posited a correspondence between the two. Although classical mechanics cannot scale down to explain the behaviour of atomic particles or waveforms, quantum mechanics can scale up to do the job of classical mechanics for large systems (so long as probability theory is also involved).

The accident investigators of the Health and Safety Laboratory ignore the reality of quantum mechanics. They work to rehabilitate classical mechanics after its legitimacy has been thrown into public doubt by industrial disasters. Their operational limit is no less than the limit of classical mechanics – which is effectively the large molecule. This explains why the lab contains experts in nano-mechanics. These scientists apply the science of mechanics at the molecular level. Instead of being concerned with the large-scale mechanical engineering of bridges and tunnels, they get to grips with the chemical engineering of nano-materials for things like cosmetics and tyres.

The lab's accident investigators take the whole domain of classical mechanics as their operational niche. They constantly return to its founding laws of motion and tentatively probe the limits of their jurisdiction. At the same time, they inhabit a world which is more completely explained by a scaled-up version of quantum mechanics. The quantum reality which drops out of their operations defines the margin for an alternative interpretation of their work.

To say that the simulations of accident investigation have affinities with the practices of sympathetic magic is one thing. It is an analogy. The most which can be claimed is that if the science of classical mechanics is tested often enough, then its historic origins become steadily more visible, and it starts to be ghosted by the earlier understanding of mechanics as a science of invisible influences.

However, quantum mechanics is quite capable of explaining the phenomenon of action at a distance so crucial to sympathetic magic. When two particles are subject to quantum entanglement, then they remain linked even when separated in space. There is a correspondence in their behaviour at the quantum level. Affect one particle and you affect the other in exactly the same fashion, even when many miles away.

If the fatal trauma of an accident were enough to make its constellating particles more susceptible to quantum entanglement, then perhaps the idea of the lab's accident investigators performing a kind of voodoo science is not quite so far-fetched. This is especially so given that there is a species of subatomic particle – the tachyon – that is known to travel backwards in time.

THERE ARE MANY SACRIFICES

The simulations of accident investigation tend to include effigies of victims in order to deliver the best results. When train crashes are reenacted, the impact of flying shards of metal on human bodies needs to be tested. The imitation of a tunnel collapse or a bridge failure similarly requires the inclusion of human equivalents to be really useful.

The Health and Safety Lab uses mannequins and plastic facsimiles of human body parts in its tests. Its accident investigators, for example, might end up setting fire to the simulacrum of a human hand in order to evaluate the relative safety of electrical equipment. The lab's craftsmen have discovered that a reliable imitation of human flesh can be created from plasticine covered in chammy leather.

In the pubs and clubs of Buxton, some distance from Harpur Hill, where the faint wail of the lab's siren can sometimes be heard on a still night, people talk of the animal tests conducted at the lab. These stories lag behind the times. The lab's accident investigators have not used animal cultures in their tests for many years. They have ethical scruples about causing animals pain.

It is no longer judged necessary to sacrifice animals in order to conduct valid investigations of accidents. Collections of rags and children's playthings are deemed sufficient as offerings.

There was never a time when it was thought productive to use human test subjects in imitations of fatal accidents. Human sacrifice belongs more properly to the pre-Christian era.

Back in Buxton, the teenage boys meet up to share the photographs they have taken of themselves inside the grounds of the lab on Harpur Hill. They have climbed on top of the rounded surface of the overground tunnel and posed in front of the underground roadway. These self-styled "urban explorers" are eager to mark the territory of a site which has the aura of a forbidden place.

The lads share tales of how they have passed along the public footpaths into Harpur Hill and then stepped off the trail, dodging the lab's security guards, laughing and joking, finding the test beds and trials

28

areas from which they are excluded for their own safety. These boys are imagined by the security guards to have an affinity with terrorists and these old men have been known to pick up the phone to Special Branch.

The urban explorers tell stories of the London Underground tube trains they found in a shallow valley on Harpur Hill. The carriages were buckled and burned. Some of the boys, in a prophecy of the return of the Church of Albion, claim to have seen charred mannequins lying on the ground. They were dressed in anoraks and had back-packs, just like the suicide bombers active on the London Underground in 2005.

FOURTH OF THE SEVEN PLACES

On the fourth stop of his tour of the Seven Wonders of the Peak, Hobbes travelled through the Peak Forest, which in those days was a deer park owned by the king, until he arrived at Eldon Hill. In the side of the hill was a gash, a deep and wide sink-hole whose sloping edge supported a few thin saplings. This was Eldon Hole.

Hobbes characterises Eldon Hole in his poem as a desolate place. This was seen by local settlers as the haunt of ghosts and demons, the beginning of a long, treacherous descent to the underworld, a zone capable of disturbing the minds of those who did not know it.

29

Hobbes describes a visit made to Eldon Hole some years earlier by an Elizabethan courtier. This lord wanted to know how deep the pit was and so paid a local man to be lowered down it in a basket. As the rope was played out yard by yard, the man's cries became fainter and fainter, until he could no longer be heard. When the basket was eventually raised back up, the man was wild-eyed, pale and trembling. He had lost his voice and he died within a week.

Hobbes was more cautious in his approach to sounding the depths of Eldon Hole. He crept to the edge and lay down with his head over the chasm. He then dropped a rough stone into the hole and listened to it bouncing off the rocks as it fell. He counted 11 knocking sounds, each fainter than the last, until he could hear no more.

The lead miners of the Peak could have advised Hobbes on

how to interpret the echoes and reverberations obtained from his dropped stone. They could have told him about the Tommyknockers, briefed him on the folklore, introduced him to another deity quite apart from Leviathan.

Certainly for the footpads and travellers of the Peak, Eldon Hole was a familiar place. It was where the bodies of murder victims could be dropped and left to rot, where the remains of unwanted pregnancies (and things more dreadful than that) could be made to disappear. It was a chamber where desperate men and women, who might well have reclaimed their natural freedoms in moments of sovereign abandon, could safely dispose of the evidence of their crimes.

Eldon Hole is still there today, its wild perimeter guarded by a thin wire fence. It has its contemporary petitioners.

TILT YARD

The Health and Safety Laboratory conducts tests into rail crashes in the wilds of Harpur Hill. The two sets of narrow gauge rail tracks are almost buried in the grass. They run from the top of a small hill down to a concrete platform attached to a low, squat viewing station. The windows of the station are dark and opaque.

The accident investigators simulate rail crashes here. A specimen truck is positioned on the track in the sunken ground near the viewing station. The siren sounds and a nine-ton hammer truck is released from the summit of the hill. It rattles down the tracks at 60 miles per hour and smashes into the stationary truck.

The force of the impact is measured by the scientists hidden in the viewing station. Often, the specimen truck will contain a tank of locomotive fuel, which has been dyed with paint so the spray pattern generated by a collision can be observed. The scientists are particularly interested in when an explosion is likely to occur.

FIFTH STOP

The fifth place which Hobbes visited on his ceremonial tour of the Peak was Tideswell. Here was the site of a mysterious well whose unpredictable ebbings and flowings were thought to be connected with the tidal pull of the moon.

There are many such wells in the Peak. They are at Buxton, Eyam, Monyash and Tissington, at Bakewell, Tansley, Cromford and Ault Hucknall. They are everywhere.

These wells are fed by hot springs from deep underground. The boiling water forces its way through the limestone rocks, coursing through the natural fissures, pummelling its way upwards, until it jets and spurts to the surface.

In his poem, Hobbes mentions how the old well was decorated with moss, grass, chaff and torn pieces of paper. He is describing the bare features of a pagan custom known as well dressing.

The wells are still dressed today in the Peak. Between late spring and early autumn, the local people take the petals and leaves of cut flowers and press them into a board of wet clay. They add rhubarb seeds, stiff alder cones, shards of tree bark and mosses and lichens to make up the face of a man.

The Green Man has been worshipped for many thousands of years. He is a memory of the vegetable god Attis, or perhaps Adonis, who dies each winter only to be resurrected in the flowers and bountiful fields of the summer. The Druidic priests of the Green Man cult were simply imitating this drama when they selected a human being to be ritually slaughtered every year. They

30

believed that the lucky victim would be transformed into a little piece of the deity. The idea was that the human sacrifice would provoke the quickening of the divine sacrifice through a process of sympathetic magic.

The Church of Albion has always had a deep respect for the cult of the Green Man.

PRIVATE CHAPEL

Crouched in the grounds of the Health and Safety Laboratory is the dust explosion facility. This large steel sphere rests on four squat legs. It has stairs leading up one side to loading hoppers at the top. The vessel is hinged so that one rounded half can swing open like a front door. The dark cavity revealed is big enough for a man to hide inside.

This piece of equipment is used to test the kinds of dust explosions which occur in the pipes and valves of factories. There is always a high risk of explosion with fine powders and dusts. Organic and metallic materials are particularly combustible. They include substances such as corn flour, custard powder and, most notoriously, coal dust.

The dust needs something to burn in before it can explode. That's why dust dispersed in the air is more explosive than dust on the ground. When a mote of dust is lifted up off the ground, it has oxygen all around it and so can burn very easily.

The dust explosion vessel is similar in its operation to the overground tunnel which travels much of the length of the lab's grounds. This tunnel was used up until the end of the 1970s to recreate the kinds of coal dust explosions likely to occur in the mines.

The same procedure was always followed. Engineers would spread an even layer of coal dust on the floor of the tunnel, using a trolley which ran on tracks. They would then set an explosive charge at one end, close the blast door and ignite the charge. The pressure wave from the resulting explosion would puff air ahead of it as it moved down the tunnel, lifting up the coal dust so that by the time the flames from the explosion arrived, there was coal dust in the air ready to burn and the fire could simply carry on propagating itself.

The same chain reaction occurs in a real coal mine – except

that here the coal dust is deposited as a result of the industrial process and the explosion occurs accidentally.

There is also in the grounds of the lab a more faithful and less adaptable simulation of a coal mining tunnel. This is the underground roadway, a real-life tunnel which has been driven through solid rock. It has long been obsolete. A red-and-white striped plastic safety barrier guards its entrance.

On the other side of the world, in China, where coal mining is an emerging industry, many thousands of people are killed in tunnels every year.

GROUND INTO ATOMS

The Health and Safety Laboratory's explosions trials are informed by a philosophical approach to matter. The core idea of this philosophy is that any material, sufficiently finely divided, can explode.

The explosiveness of granulated matter is attested to not only by combustible dust deposits, but also by fuel-air mixes and the agitations of hydrogen gas. It is when matter is in a molecular state that its explosiveness is most clearly demonstrated.

The lab tests the limits of the explosiveness of matter in its work with nano-materials. These very fine molecules offer definite fire and explosion hazards once they are airborne.

31

Inside the electronically sealed doors of the lab is the room containing the nano-materials explosion device. This is a two-litre size steel sphere, distant cousin of the much larger dust explosion vessel in the grounds outside. Here is where the lab's scientists test the explosion characteristics of a range of nano-materials, from aluminium and iron to carbon and copper.

The nano-materials are injected into the vessel at atmospheric pressure. An electrical igniter reaches down into the centre of the vessel. It is clicked and a spark jumps into the air. The molecules start to burn and the nano-cloud erupts into an explosion lasting tens of milliseconds.

If there are too many or too few nano-particles in the air, they will fail to explode. That is because it is not the number of molecules in the air which is critical to their explosiveness – it is their exposed surface area. When particles are suspended in the air, they exhibit Brownian motion or random fluctuation. This movement excites the electrical charge between mutually exposed molecules and explosive pressure mounts.

It was the ancient Greek philosopher Lucretius who proposed that the universe was composed of atoms in the void. When the atoms fall in straight lines, then nothing ever changes and the eternal presence of God may be inferred. When the atoms begin to deviate from their straight lines, then there is the possibility for connection and collision. The space of Newtonian mechanics emerges and the Hobbesian social contract can take place.

Lucretius indicates that the limit of this swerving tendency once it has got going is the mutual repulsion of atoms in the void. Here is where random fluctuation intensifies, vortices begin to form, and Newtonian mechanics loses its bearings. Under such circumstances, the Hobbesian state teeters on the edge of implosion. The political question which then arises is – does the anarchy of sovereign atoms have to mean social conflagration and civil war?

"WAR OF ALL AGAINST ALL"

Thomas Hobbes is not nowadays in fashion as a political philosopher. He is thought too attached to the sovereignty of the state. The Italian anarchist philosopher Paolo Virno makes a typical effort to deconstruct Hobbes. He observes that the Hobbesian social contract delivers a unified "people" from a dissenting "multitude". For Hobbes, the multitude is a negative entity which fails to transfer its natural rights to the sovereign. It is warring, fractious, does not enter into lasting agreements and resists political authority. Virno seizes on the idea of the multitude and tries to give it a positive spin. He agrees with Hobbes that the multitude shuns the state monopoly of political decision-making. But he does not see them reduced to war. Instead, there is a celebration of "plurality".

There is an idea of the multitude as a collective social body composed of migrants, exiles, dissidents, outlaws, criminals and paupers. These carnival figures are never a unified people. They have no property, no land, no settled nation. Instead, they have the freedom of perpetual vagabondage.

This multitude is always welcome at the Church of Albion.

The Peak District was once full of gypsies, who travelled in horse-drawn wagons, speaking their own language or cant, living by their own customs, mistrusted by the people among whom they moved. These outsider tribes passed through nations without putting down roots, their caravans stretching across continents. They were made up of knife-grinders, rag-and-bone men, hawkers, dealers in second-hand goods, fairground people, knackers, tinkers and the odd sheep stealer.

In Hobbes's time (and up until the late eighteenth century), gypsies were subject to a punitive criminal code which included the death penalty. The Peak was a place where they could hide out from the authorities. Gypsies squatted old barns, moved into caves and jumped over drystone walls to set up tents or "benders" in the fields.

The Church of England refused to accept gypsies. The

travelling multitude buried their dead at the roadside. The wayside graves are still visible at Beeley, Ladybower, Hathersage, Sheldon and Pilsley.

Gypsies were often mythologised by peasants uncertain of their leases and industrial workers crammed into factories. They became symbols of a collective dream for a world free of capitalist exploitation, oppression and isolation. It's a familiar story. The idea of the outsider has always been more important for people than have the outsiders themselves.

32

LOCATION NUMBER SIX

Hobbes began his journey through the Peak District at Chatsworth, his lord's household. He then travelled into the wilds. The last two stops on his tour were both located in Buxton. So when he rode into the spa town with his companions, battered, weary, slightly road-crazed, he would have been eager to reacquaint himself with the comforts of a settled lifestyle.

The sixth of the Seven Wonders of the Peak visited by Hobbes was St Anne's Well. Buxton's heated spring-fed waters had been celebrated for their restorative properties since the Roman occupation. The waters of St Anne's Well were thought to have healing powers and the old and the infirm were accustomed to bathe in them.

33

In Hobbes's time, the ancient well was more like a large square-shaped hot tub. It was five feet deep and screened by walls and a roof. Access was through the door of a neighbouring inn. Hobbes describes how he and his fellows stripped off their travelling gear before lowering themselves into the bath.

Is there a memory of the Green Man cult here? It is said that the men and women sacrificed to the fertility deity were subject to strenuous rituals of purification before they were killed.

St Anne's Well is still there in Buxton today. Now it supplies only drinking water.

OLD GALLOWS

In the grounds of the Health and Safety Laboratory is an edifice known as a drop test rig. Its main component is a 25 metre high tower fashioned from steel girders. Attached to it is the horizontal arm of a crane which can slide up and down. The whole is surrounded by a square platform of wooden planks, with a staircase up one side.

Accidents involving drops and falls are tested here. Materials such as concrete beams and aluminium panels are secured to the end of the crane. The whole beam can then be subjected to sudden and extreme vertical displacements.

Here is where safety engineers once used to test the kind of bucket elevator drops which occurred at minehead shafts. Nowadays, the falls simulated are more likely to happen in the construction industry. The safety nets are strung up beneath the tower, and a large 100 gram sphere is dropped from the crane. The nets are tested under a range of conditions, simulating heavy rainfall, and extremes of light. The sphere stands in for the body of a construction worker. The tests are designed to discover when the nets break and the frail yellow ball hurtles through to the ground.

In another part of the lab, inside the glass walls of the thermal chamber, investigators dress the dummy heads with protective headgear and set fire to them.

SEVENTH LOCATION

On the last stop of his tour of the Seven Wonders of the Peak, Hobbes visited Poole's Cavern on the outskirts of Buxton. This large, naturally-formed cave is named after a bandit who lived there in medieval times. Hobbes describes him as a thief and murderer who lured victims to his lair before robbing and killing them. The locals prefer to think of him as a Robin Rood-like figure, who stole from the rich to give to the poor, using crime as an instant means of wealth redistribution.

The caves and pot-holes and abandoned mines lie everywhere in the Peak District. Hidden away in the hillsides, they have long offered refuge to poachers, heretics, vagrants and other fugitives of the state. They are the places which enable outlaws to drop out for a time. These are the sites where people fade from view.

34

Outside Monyash, the river Lathkill rises among the broken rocks and pushes eastwards, surging past the limestone cliffs. The men and women of the Church of Albion climbed the rocks to disappear into One Ash Shelter, Demons Dale Cave and Calling Low Dale Rock Shelter. They were hiding from the authorities, who were inclined to persecute them. Here is where a counter-strategy of lying low becomes indistinguishable from the politics of rumour. Some say the people of the Church of Albion lived in the rocks for successive generations, boring through the limestone, tunnelling underground, until they found a way to America. Others say they became ghosts.

The Peak Forest is where poachers used to run at night, armed with bow and arrow. They shot the deer which belonged to the king and took the carcass home for supper. Eldon Hole was a particularly favoured hide-out.

Meanwhile, it was gypsies and travelling peoples who hauled their caravans into the Devil's Arse. They lit fires under the cavernous limestone roof, watered their horses from the underground springs and broke out the musical instruments made of hide and bark. The droning sounds went on all night, unsettling the sleep of the townspeople in Castleton.

The old lead mines outside of Matlock Bath have been bored deep into the limestone cliff. They were exhausted of their ore many centuries ago. Fern Cave and Roman Cave were abandoned long before they came to be occupied by bandits. These desperate men used to spy on the traders coming into town from Nottingham, drop down on them and steal their wares, before disappearing back into the caves to share the spoils.

Once the common lands were enclosed at Matlock, Bonsall and Wirksworth, the peasants were turfed out on to the roads and ended up squatting Carsington Pasture Cave and Harsborough Cave. They built temporary shelters from wood and canvas and armed themselves with staves. They accepted the company of lead miners thrown out of work. And they defended themselves from the local constabulary when efforts were made to move them on.

South of the Peak at Uttoxeter is where the last battle of the English Civil War should have taken place but didn't. At the tail-end of the war in 1648, King Charles I had been captured by the New Model Army. He tried to escape final defeat by involving himself in clandestine negotiations with the Scots. The top lord of Scotland, the Marquis of Hamilton, duly raised an army. He crossed the border into England, captured Berwick, moved through Northumberland, and took Carlisle. The plan was to keep moving south.

The civil war looked as if it could flare up again. Oliver Cromwell sped through the Midlands with his troops, hooking up just north of the Peak District with another force under the command of General John Lambert, until he was able to field 9,000 men against the 20,000-strong Scots army at Preston. The battle lasted two days on a boggy terrain, where foot-soldiers were lashed by rain and mud. Many Scots were either killed or captured.

Hamilton's army had been fatally attacked in the rear. The remnants at the front continued to stagger south, harried and pursued by Lambert, until they finally surrendered at Uttoxeter without a shot being fired. Some of the defeated Scottish cavalry were locked up in the town's church. Others managed to escape the enemy, making their way to the banks of the River Dove and tracking it north upstream, back to the remote parts of the Peak District.

The defeated monarchists hid out for a time, wary of being captured by Puritan soldiers and sent in chains to the plantations of Virginia or Barbados. They discovered Fox Hole Cave in High Wheeldon and ensconced themselves inside the hill. They stumbled across the River Manifold, a tributary of the Dove, and followed it into deeper regions, bedding down in Thor's Cave, Elder Bush Cave, Ossom's Crag Cave and Thor's Fissure Cave, among memories of ancient pagan gods.

OLD GIBBET

In a relatively sheltered part of the grounds of the Health and Safety Lab, beside the still waters of an ornamental pond, there lurks the iron carcass of the warehouse fire test rig. This large-frame structure is built to simulate not just a warehouse but any cargo storage area along the logistics chain of the global economy – a heavy goods vehicle, for example, or a freighter.

The safety rig is built like an open cage and stands higher than one of the Neolithic stone henges on the Peak. Four iron girders rise up from the earth to make a square shape. There are two walls of corrugated iron sheeting hanging opposite each other. There is no roof.

The steel chains hang down from the structure and clank in the wind. The joints of the rusting iron creak and groan.

Here is where accident investigators test the rate at which combustible liquids such as oil will burn when stored under certain conditions. Fuel is nowadays transported in square-shaped 1,000 litre plastic containers. These have replaced the steel drum, because they stack more efficiently when transported.

The lab's engineers place the containers inside the rig and check the wind speed. They throw out some sparks in the vicinity of the containers – such as might happen in real life through carelessness – and monitor the results. Typically, plastic at the edge of a container will catch fire and melt, creating a hole, through which fuel vapour leaks into the surrounding air. An explosion usually happens quite quickly. It is then a matter of measuring how rapidly the fire can engulf a storage area through the spread of burning pools.

Often, the investigators will set up boundary walls between containers to discover how far this can check the spread of fire.

THE PROPHETS TELL

In the eighteenth chapter of the sacred book of the Koran, known as the "Cave", there is told the story of Gog and Magog. These destructive creatures are imprisoned behind a wall by a great king. His intention is to protect a local tribe of people, who duly offer him tribute in the customary way.

Gog and Magog never stop trying to escape from their confinement. The Koran states that their final exodus is a sign that doomsday has arrived.

In British folklore, Gog and Magog combine to form Gogmagog, last of the aboriginals who once inhabited the land. This tribe of nomads was driven into the caves by the first British king and his followers, compelled to disappear into the cracks and fissures of remote heaths by the development of farming and the occupation of the fields. Here is where they wait.

The anthropologist Pierre Clastres offers a kind of apology for Gog and Magog. He argues that indigenous tribes ward off state formation through the practices of war. There are always a number of potential leaders in a tribe, jockeying for positions of influence among their fellows. As soon as one leader looks as if he might become dominant and assume sovereign command, then the others combine to undermine his authority.

35

War is here understood as a set of social relations which preserves the distinctive composition of a small multitude. The several leaders compete with one another for status in an escalating display of expenditure, which takes on destructive aspects as amassed symbolic wealth – such as beautiful shells or highly decorated pieces of paper – is thrown down and sacrificed.

Gog and Gogmagog combat each other by impoverishing themselves in conspicuous acts of self-aggrandisement. That way, neither one of them can threaten to take over the tribe. Gogmagog is never a king. He is a crazy man, an enemy combatant, a schizophrenic. He is a true prophet of the Church of Albion.

S.B. / December 2009 / Hove

Film Documents

Voicescript

Act One

Hello. Hello. This is the Tommy Hobbes Peakland Mystery Tour. Make yourself ready.

My name is Blakey and I will be your tour guide. You get me? I am the last surviving member of the Church of Albion. Those of my congregation were all imprisoned, hanged and transported by a terrible beast named Leviathan. I myself was driven into the caves and have only now returned.

Stay awake, now.

We are in the Peak District. This massive national park in the middle of England was once owned by a single bastard family. Tommy Hobbes worked for that family as a kept scholar, tutor to their sons, a tame poet and resident prostitute of the mind.

Now we are on his trail.

Keep your eyes open for military aircraft wrecks, collapsed mine shafts and prehistoric burial mounds.

Now, you may think you know about Thomas Hobbes. You may think, yes, he is the man who invented the idea of the social contract back in the old days. He is the man who said that once you have surrendered to the state, you no longer have the right to settle your own scores. The state does it for you, with its army of lawyers.

But I'm not talking about Thomas Hobbes the political philosopher, the old white guy from the Royal Society you read about in school. Get that idea right out of your head. I'm talking about Tommy Hobbes the magic man, the fucking voodoo scientist, right?

Tommy Hobbes programmed the operating system of the British state from his text terminal. This spectre took the form of a giant artificial man, a king. Tommy coded the entity so that it swallows up all those men and women who bend the knee to it. Tommy reckoned this creature was a monster and he named it Leviathan.

You get me? The British state is the beast Leviathan. It is as the prophets of the Church of Albion say – "we saw a cataract of blood mixed with fire, and not many stones' throw from us appeared and sunk again the scaly fold of a monstrous serpent."

Watch it, now.

Long ago, people in this neck of the woods worshipped a deity known as the Green Man. In fact, they were so enthralled, they used to sacrifice a young man or woman to him every year.

Here we are at Ault Hucknall. Tommy is supposed to be buried in the parish church, though I tell you now that the sorcerer faked his own death and is alive and well, still minded to persecute those of my church.

As for Albion, he is a poor giant who sleeps on a stone.

Follow me now. Listen.

What I'm saying is that Tommy Hobbes, insomniac and astrologer, came down from his watchtower one night and went deep into the Peak. He travelled to seven different places, all owned by his employer, the king's local mob boss, and he dug into the limestone to gather seven bucketloads of clay.

Back in his laboratory, Tommy slaps these great lumps of mud together to make a statue of a giant man. He writes some Egyptian algorithms on slips of paper, slots them into the joints of the creature, and waits a few minutes. Bingo! The artificial man opens his eyes. He is animated by the power of assembly code.

Tommy names his golem Leviathan Two. He does this because the creature is a copy, at a massively reduced scale, of the original Leviathan.

So say the prophets of Albion, who were living in that time.

Act Two

I will now conduct you on a tour of the seven locations from which Tommy dug out the materials for his golem. Are you ready?

The first stop on the tour.

Here we have reached the country pile of Leviathan Two. This is where Tommy keeps his pet monster.

The old magician, still alive, alerts Leviathan Two when the police send him word of large-scale accidents which have damaged the integrity of the British state. We are talking rail crashes, tunnel collapses, industrial fires and explosions. Get me? The kind of thing that happens two or three hundred times a year. The kind of thing that kills four hundred or so people. Four hundred people a year, okay?

Leviathan Two appears at the site of the accident, his mouth sealed tightly shut, and he collects the debris. Then, it's back, invisible as night to his hidden stately home, where he stashes the evidence safe behind drystone walls.

36

It's there, beneath the radar of a no-fly zone; so much twisted metal, worn nuts and bolts, a piece of a nuclear sub, concrete powder, melted iron. It's all there.

This is the second tour location, the great hall within the house of Leviathan Two.

Here, the clay golem patiently brings out the debris of an

accident for his master Tommy to inspect. Tommy places the remains of Leviathan on a steel floor, sorting them into different patterns. He knows in principle what has occurred. There has been a visitation. Gogmagog, demon of chaos, has hit upon Leviathan in the dark, inflicting grievous bodily harm. But what is the exact nature of the wounding?

Tommy instructs Leviathan Two to perform the golem trick of raising the dead to give testimony. The artificial man complies. He waves his master's remote control and those killed in the accident return, as ghosts, to stand behind a yellow line painted on the floor. Their voices are as rain in the night.

Tommy has all the information he needs. He conjures a scenario to explain the accident. Leviathan was here, in this position, exposed in such a way. Gogmagog intervened here, and here. Tommy gets Leviathan Two to act out the scenario. The artificial man submits. He is dropped to the floor from a crane, he is hung with weights, he is punched and holed. Tommy examines the debris. He is looking for a scale match with the original debris from Leviathan himself.

Finally, Tommy has it. He nods to himself. The scenario has passed the test. From here, it enters into law and becomes reality.

We now go from the house of Leviathan Two into the extensive grounds. There are flowers of great beauty, not otherwise seen beyond Siberia.

This is the winding path of which the prophets say: "Roses are planted where thorns grow / And on the barren heath / Sing the honey bees."

We have now arrived at the hunting lodge of Leviathan Two, third stop on the tour. Here, inside the control room, is where Tommy performs his most delicate work. Making certain gestures, manipulating certain objects, he conjures Gogmagog and binds him to the winding path.

Leviathan Two is staked out as a token sacrifice. Tommy finds the magic words and his imitation of the beast Leviathan is consumed by the anger of Gogmagog.

The operation begins. It is as the prophets say: "Gogmagog roars and shakes his fires in the burdened air / Hungry clouds swag on the deep."

There is a deal in place. It has a pre-emptive character. By imitating the event he fears and offering this substitute to Gogmagog, Tommy hopes to stave off the real event and prevent it from ever happening.

This is ultimately a legal matter. Tommy is marking the boundaries between Leviathan and Gogmagog, between order and chaos. Do you follow? Again, the prophets have it when they tell the story of how the king Leviathan imprisoned the monster Gogmagog behind a wall of stones.

Tommy is constantly having to reassemble his clay man. There are many terrible scenarios of Leviathan's destruction to be acted out. There are many sacrifices to be made to Gogmagog.

Tommy is testing the limits of his concept of the state. You see, he first coded Leviathan back in the days of the English Civil War. He is painfully aware of the flimsiness of his original creation.

The man is suffering from obsessive compulsive disorder.

The fourth of the seven places where Tommy found clay for his golem.

Tommy has cut Leviathan Two in half and, as with a giant worm, the two halves have grown to become doubles of each other. Two versions of the same artificial man. Terrible

37

twins.

Here, at the tilt yard, Tommy pits the twin versions of Leviathan Two against each other. He is casting out the spirit of civil war. Gogmagog attends. There is always much noise and chaos for the demon to feed upon.

This is the fifth stop on the tour.

Here, at the private chapel, Tommy conducts his most extreme performance. Leviathan Two has been pulverised, ground into atoms. The fine powder is deposited on the floor of the chapel, where Gogmagog awaits. The door is shut. Ignition takes place.

Tommy is guided by an alchemical principle. He figures that any social body, sufficiently granulated, returns to the original explosive state of cosmic matter. He calls this primal scene the "war of all against all". It is the event he is most anxious to ward off.

Now, the Church of Albion has always disputed this principle. We believe that the universe is ruled not by war but by love. We believe that once the beast Leviathan is disassembled, a new society of friendship and mutual cooperation will flourish in its place.

We say that Leviathan is nothing more than the giant Albion in a state of sleep. We say that the British state is nothing more

than a bad dream from which we all must awake.

Now, you can see that under this changed way of looking at things, Gogmagog is no demon of chaos but instead an angel of enlightenment. Gogmagog is here to give us a wake-up call. We now have a chance to cast off the beast Leviathan and discover the loving powers of Albion.

38

Here is location number six.

We are now at the site of the old gallows.

Here is a dreadful place. Leviathan Two would climb on the scaffold to string up an outlaw before a sample crowd. The outlaw would naturally resist his fate and there would be a struggle. The question for Tommy was - how far could this struggle go before the crowd pitched in on the side of the outlaw? Various scenarios were conjured. Gogmagog was invited to feed upon spectacles of civil disorder.

Tommy never really managed to protect Leviathan from the mob at the scaffold. It is the case that the gallows is no longer used by the British state. Other, less hazardous methods have been found to punish the outlaw.

We arrive at the seventh location.

Here, we see another disused part of the country estate of Leviathan Two. It is the site of the old gibbet.

This is where Tommy continued his experiments. He would instruct Leviathan Two, his enforcer, to take the corpse of the hanged outlaw and exhibit it inside an iron cage suspended at the side of the road. The golem obeyed his master but first covered the dead body in thick tar to prevent it from decomposing.

Tommy was concerned with but one issue. For how long would random passers-by on the road consent to be intimidated before they fired the corpse?

The heat given off by this magical action was always most gratifying to Gogmagog.

Again, Tommy's spell was ineffective. The gibbet always risked too much in the way of popular defiance of the British state. It was eventually taken down.

Act Three

Now we leave the estate of Leviathan Two. The Tommy Hobbes Peakland Mystery Tour is nearing its end. You have seen with your own eyes the seven places where Tommy discovered the clay for his golem. You have given a hearing to Blakey, your tour guide, last of his church.

There is one final stop on the tour.

We are travelling back. Back to the house built by Tommy's boss.

This is the secret watchtower of Tommy Hobbes. Every night, without exception, the ancient magician, his flesh stiffened with various elixirs, climbs the steps to his laboratory in the sky. From here, he surveys the movement of the stars and calculates the fate of the kingdom.

Tommy keeps a small altar to Gogmagog in his laboratory. He thinks it is as well to stay on good terms with one's demons. The effigy of Gogmagog stands above a fireplace and is covered.

What do the prophets tell of Gogmagog? They tell that he was secured behind a wall of stones by the king Leviathan. What else do the prophets say? They say that every night, the demon works to tear down the wall, stone by stone. As dawn breaks, he has created a gap the size of a fist. But then, each dusk as he returns, the hole has been sealed by the command of Leviathan.

Gogmagog keeps on working every night to breach the wall, and he will keep on working through many centuries, until Leviathan accepts he is no more than the dream of Albion, who sleeps on a stone. At that time, Gogmagog will break through the wall of stones and rush

39

headlong through the land.

Many years ago, human sacrifice took place in the Peak.

There is no more to say.

Credits

Voodoo Science Park

a film by
Victoria Halford & Steve Beard

voice
Jeff Noon

original music
Scanner

consulting editor
Steve Lewis

commissioned by
The Arts Catalyst and SCAN

shot on location at
the Health and Safety Laboratory (HSL) in the Peak District
National Park, Derbyshire

thanks to
Eddie Morland, Karen Wilkinson, Phil Heyes and Steve
Graham from HSL

thanks also to
Robert White, Richard Bettis, Stuart Hawksworth, Michael
Stewart, Nichola Stacey, Duncan Webb, Nicholas Vaughan,
Jacqui Patel, Liz Brueck, Graham Atkinson, Matt Birtles, Peter
Ellwood and Dave Mark from HSL

Picture Credits

Pictures are photos taken by the authors, unless stated otherwise.

01: Armoured window shutters of a control building in the grounds of the Health and Safety Laboratory (HSL).

02: Side entrance into HSL.

03: Sign at HSL.

04: Testing rig in the grounds of HSL.

05: Interior of dummy gas canister at HSL.

06: Inside the overground tunnel at HSL.

07: Plaque on the wall of the church at Ault Hucknall. It commemorates one of the gamekeepers employed by the Cavendish family.

08: Pressure gauges dial at HSL.

09: Sign on tree directing traffic to the church at Ault Hucknall.

10: Mannequin racked outside the thermal lab at HSL.

11: Figure in high visibility jacket at HSL.

12: Thomas Hobbes's title page engraving for his book, *Leviathan*. The image is in the public domain.

13: Radio tower next to HSL control building.

14: Narrow gauge rail tracks in the grounds of HSL.

15: Interior of the incident lab at HSL.

16: The top of the entrance to the underground roadway in the grounds of HSL.

17: Fire engulfment pit at HSL.

18: One of the exhibits at the Peak District Mining Museum in Matlock Bath.

19: Dummy heads on a shelf outside the thermal chamber at HSL.

20: Interior of the hut (known locally as "Grim's Drift") built into the wall of HSL's underground roadway.

21: Abandoned testing material in the grounds of HSL.

22: Testing equipment at the fire engulfment pit at HSL.

23: Sign at HSL.

24: Drop test rig in the grounds of HSL.

25: Warehouse fire test rig (known locally as "the temple of doom") in the grounds of HSL.

26: Illustrated plate from William Blake's *Europe*. The image is in the public domain.

27: Scene from a vehicle test fire in the forecourt of HSL.

28: Overground tunnel in the grounds of HSL.

29: The double doors which open into HSL's anechoic chamber.

30: Signs painted on the floor of HSL's incident lab.

31: Sign at HSL.

32: Disused rail track in the grounds of HSL.

33: Landscaped pond next to the warehouse fire test rig at HSL.

34: Entrance to the underground roadway in the grounds of HSL.

35: Acoustic wedges on the interior wall of HSL's anechoic chamber.

36: King's Cross station on the London Underground in the aftermath of the fire of 1987. The image is Crown copyright and used with the kind permission of HSL.

37: Train collision test using scale model rolling stock. The image is Crown copyright and used with the kind permission of HSL.

38: Coal dust explosion test at the overground tunnel in the grounds of HSL. The image is Crown copyright and used with the kind permission of HSL.

39: Interior of train carriage at moment of impact during crash test. The image is Crown copyright and used with the kind permission of HSL.

Source Books

Giorgio Agamben, *Remnants of Auschwitz* (MIT Press, 2002)

Walter Benjamin, *One-Way Street and Other Writings* (Penguin Classics, 2009)

William Blake, *The Complete Poems* (Penguin Classics, 2004)

Pierre Clastres, *Archeology of Violence* (Semiotext(e), 1994)

Michel de Certeau, *The Practice of Everyday Life* (University of California Press, 2002)

T. D. Ford and J. H. Rieuwerts, *Lead Mining in the Peak District* (Peak District Mines Historical Society Ltd, 2000)

Michel Foucault, *Discipline and Punish* (Penguin Social Sciences, 1991)

Christopher Hill, *Puritanism and Revolution* (Pimlico, 2001)

Thomas Hobbes, *De Mirabilibus Pecci: being the wonders of the Peak in Darby-shire* (London, 1678)

Thomas Hobbes, *Leviathan* (Oxford World's Classics, 2008)

Lucretius, *The Nature of Things* (Penguin Classics, 2007)

Carl Schmitt, *The Concept of the Political*, with Notes by Leo Strauss (Chicago University Press, 2007)

Keith Thomas, *Religion and the Decline of Magic* (Penguin History, 2003)

Paul Virilio, *Unknown Quantity* (Thames & Hudson, 2003)

Paolo Virno, *A Grammar of the Multitude* (Semiotext(e), 2004)

Acknowledgements

This book would not exist without the making of the film. And the film would not exist without the support and encouragement of Helen Sloan from SCAN and Nicola Triscott, Rob La Frenais and Gillean Dickie from The Arts Catalyst.

Many people contributed to this book apart from the authors.

Our biggest debt of thanks is owed to the people at the Health and Safety Laboratory who gave us the benefit of their expertise on our visits there in 2007. In particular, we should mention Phil Heyes, one of the lab's leading mechanical engineers. His knowledge and generosity were quite simply outstanding.

Our thanks are also due to Tony Bell, who conducted us on a tour of the church at Ault Hucknall at literally two hours' notice. Reverend Bell was concerned to emphasise that Thomas Hobbes accepted the Christian host upon his death-bed and was therefore not an atheist.

We are also grateful to Stewart Home for writing such a great foreword at such short notice. The man is a true star.

Finally, we should thank Tariq Goddard, Emma Stewart, Mark Fisher, Trevor Greenfield, Stuart Davies and the team at Zer0 Books for their understanding, commitment and dedication. No book could have hoped for a better crew.

Any mistakes or misunderstandings in this book are quite naturally those of the authors alone.

Contemporary culture has eliminated both the concept of the public and the figure of the intellectual. Former public spaces – both physical and cultural – are now either derelict or colonized by advertising. A cretinous anti-intellectualism presides, cheerled by expensively educated hacks in the pay of multinational corporations who reassure their bored readers that there is no need to rouse themselves from their interpassive stupor. The informal censorship internalized and propagated by the cultural workers of late capitalism generates a banal conformity that the propaganda chiefs of Stalinism could only ever have dreamt of imposing. Zer0 Books knows that another kind of discourse – intellectual without being academic, popular without being populist – is not only possible: it is already flourishing, in the regions beyond the striplit malls of so-called mass media and the neurotically bureaucratic halls of the academy. Zer0 is committed to the idea of publishing as a making public of the intellectual. It is convinced that in the unthinking, blandly consensual culture in which we live, critical and engaged theoretical reflection is more important than ever before.